6

Life

SECOND EDITION

NATIONAL GEOGRAPHIC
LEARNING

PAUL DUMMETT
DAVID BOHLKE

Australia · Brazil · Mexico · Singapore · United Kingdom · United States

NATIONAL GEOGRAPHIC
L E A R N I N G

Life 6 Workbook, **Second Edition**
Paul Dummett, David Bohlke

Vice President, Editorial Director:
John McHugh

Publisher: Andrew Robinson

Senior Development Editor: Derek Mackrell

Editorial Assistant: Dawne Law

Director of Global Marketing: Ian Martin

Senior Product Marketing Manager:
Caitlin Thomas

Media Researcher: Rebecca Ray,
Leila Hishmeh

Senior IP Analyst: Alexandra Ricciardi

IP Project Manager: Carissa Poweleit

Senior Director, Production:
Michael Burggren

Production Manager: Daisy Sosa

Content Project Manager: Beth McNally

Manufacturing Planner:
Mary Beth Hennebury

Art Director: Brenda Carmichael

Cover Design: Lisa Trager

Text Design: emc design ltd.

Compositor: DoubleInk Publishing Services

For product information and technology assistance, contact us at
Cengage Learning Customer & Sales Support, cengage.com/contact

For permission to use material from this text or product, submit all requests online at **cengage.com/permissions**
Further permissions questions can be emailed to
permissionrequest@cengage.com

ISBN: 978-1-337-90798-9

National Geographic Learning
20 Channel Center Street
Boston, MA 02210
USA

National Geographic Learning, a Cengage Learning Company, has a mission to bring the world to the classroom and the classroom to life. With our English language programs, students learn about their world by experiencing it. Through our partnerships with National Geographic and TED Talks, they develop the language and skills they need to be successful global citizens and leaders.

Locate your local office at **international.cengage.com/region**

Visit National Geographic Learning online at **NGL.Cengage.com/ELT**
Visit our corporate website at **www.cengage.com**

CREDITS

Text:
We are grateful to the following for permission to reproduce copyright material:

Extract from *Dumbing Down Our Kids: Why American Children feel good about themselves but can't read, write or add,* copyright © 1995 by Charles J. Sykes. Reprinted by permission of St. Martin's Press. All rights reserved; National Geographic for extracts adapted from 'Tibet's Golden 'Worm'' by Michael Finkel, August 2012, http://ngm.nationalgeographic.com; Interview with Daniel Raven-Ellison http://www.nationalgeographic.com; 'Sky caves of Nepal' by, Michael Finkel, October 2012, http://ngm.nationalgeographic.com; 'The City Solution' by Robert Kunzig, NG Magazine, December 2011http://ngm.nationalgeographic.com; 'Here comes the sun' by Peter McBride, National Geographic Traveler, October 2012, http://travel.nationalgeographic.com/travel/countries/india-yoga-traveler/; 'I Found the Bones of the *Bounty*' by Luis Marden, December 1957, http://ngm.nationalgeographic.com/1957/12/pitcairn-island/marden-text; http://www.nationalgeographic.com/explorers/bios/albert-lin/; 'Interview with Jake Shimabukuro' by Amina Ragheb, 22 March 2011, http://worldmusic.nationalgeographic.com; 'Interview with Marie Arana' by Melissa Wiley, 2007. http://ngm.nationalgeographic.com; and 'The New Oil Landscape The fracking frenzy in North Dakota has boosted the U.S. fuel supply—but at what cost?' by Edwin Dobb, NGM, March 2013, http://ngm.nationalgeographic.com, copyright © National Geographic. Reproduced with permission; Daniel Raven-Ellison for an interview adapted from text on www.nationalgeographic.com. Reproduced with kind permission; Chimurenga Magzine for an extract from http://www.pilgrimages.org.za. Reproduced with permission; Jake Shimabukuro for an interview adapted from text on http://worldmusic.nationalgeographic.com. Reproduced with kind permission; Interview with Marie Arana by Melissa Wiley. Reproduced by kind permission of Marie Arana, author of the memoir 'American Chica,' the novel 'Cellophane', and the biography 'Bolívar: American Liberator'; Perseus Books Group for an extract from *Mighty Be Our Powers* by Leymah Gbowee, p.102, Beast Books, September 2011. Reproduced with permission; ACE - African Conservation Experience for an extract based on details on Phinda Game Reserve, www.conservationafrica.net/projects/phinda-wildlife-research-project. Reproduced with kind permission; Guardian News & Media Ltd for an extract adapted from 'Why the Scottish wildcat is staring extinction in the face' by Robin McKie in *The Observer* 16 September 2012, copyright © Guardian News & Media Ltd, 2012.

Cover: © Francois Nel/Getty Images.

Photos: 4 © Halfpoint/Shutterstock.com; 6 © Dan Westergren/National Geographic Creative; 8 Mike Booth/Alamy Stock Photo; 9 Tony Tallec/Alamy Stock Photo; 10 © Andrey_Popov/Shutterstock.com; 12 © Kevin Frayer/Stringer/Getty Images; 14 © Gary John Norman/Getty Images; 16 © Daniel Raven-Ellison; 17 © aslysun/Shutterstock.com; 19 (l) © Sasha Leahovcenco; 19 (m) Hemis/Alamy Stock Photo; 19 (r) © Tim Matsui/Liaison/Getty Images; 20 (t) Kumar Sriskandan/Alamy Stock Photo; 20 (b) david sanger photography/Alamy Stock Photo; 22 © Richard I'Anson/Getty Images; 24 (l) © funkyfrogstock/Shutterstock.com; 24 (m) © mambo6435/Shutterstock.com; 24 (r) © EcoPrint/Shutterstock.com; 25 imageBROKER/Alamy Stock Photo; 26 © oblong1/Shutterstock.com; 28 © Gene Blevins/AFP/Getty Images; 30 © Bill Pugliano/Stringer/Getty Images; 31 Matthew Ecker / Alamy Stock Photo; 32 Asia Images Group Pte Ltd/Alamy Stock Photo; 33 © Fuse/Getty Images; 36 Justin Kase zsixz/Alamy Stock Photo; 40 Sergey Uryadnikov/Alamy Stock Photo; 41 © Peter Kim/Dreamstime.com; 42 © Luciano Mortula/Shutterstock.com; 43 © Mauricio Abreu/Getty Images; 44 © Peter McBride/National Geographic Creative; 45 MediaWorldImages/Alamy Stock Photo; 46 © Ljupco Smokovski/Shutterstock.com; 48 GoGo Images Corporation/Alamy Stock Photo; 49 © ArtmannWitte/Shutterstock.com; 50 © Mike Flippo/Shutterstock.com; 52 © Hans Verleur Photo & Film/Getty Images; 53 © Luciano Mortula/Shutterstock.com; 54 UniversalPhotography/Alamy Stock Photo; 55 Paul Price/Alamy Stock Photo; 56 Niels van Kampenhout/Alamy Stock Photo; 57 © Tino Soriano/National Geographic Creative; 58 (t) Joern Koehler/dpa picture alliance archive/Alamy Stock Photo; 58 (b) © Tim Laman/National Geographic Creative; 59 © http://selfiecity.net, Dr. Lev Manovich, Noritz Stefaner, Dr. Mehrdad Yazdani, Dr. Dominikus Baur, Jay Chow, Daniel Goddemeyer, Alise Tifentale, Nadav Hochman, 2014; 60 Craig Lovell/Eagle Visions Photography/Alamy Stock Photo; 62 © Joe Klamar/AFP/Getty Images; 63 © Ronald Sumners/Shutterstock.com; 64 © Jan Persson/Redferns/Getty Images; 65 © Pavel L Photo and Video/Shutterstock.com; 66 © William Albert Allard/National Geographic Creative; 68 Juice Images/Alamy Stock Photo; 70 Juergen Hasenkopf/Alamy Stock Photo; 71 Huw Jones/Alamy Stock Photo; 72 © Luis Marden/National Geographic Creative; 73 Ken Welsh/Alamy Stock Photo; 74 (t) INTERFOTO/Alamy Stock Photo; 74 (b) GL Archive/Alamy Stock Photo; 75 (tl) © Jim Richardson/National Geographic Creative; 75 (tr) Science History Images/Alamy Stock Photo; 75 (bl) © Amy Toensing/National Geographic Creative; 76 © Peter Betts/Shutterstock.com; 78 Piter Lenk / Alamy Stock Photo; 80 © Amanda Schwab/StarPix/REX/Shutterstock.com; 81 Jeff Morgan 16/Alamy Stock Photo; 82 © Toshiyuki Aizawa/Bloomberg/Getty Images; 83 (t) Cheryl Ann Quigley/Shutterstock.como; 83 (ml) © John McEvoy; 83 (mr) © B. Yen; 83 (bl) © Jason Edwards/National Geographic Creative; 83 (br) © Matthieu Paley/National Geographic Creative; 84 © Holly Harris/Getty Images; 86 © Rob Wilson/Shutterstock.com; 88 © Eliza Grinnell, Harvard SEAS Communications/Harvard School of Engineering and Applied Sciences; 89 © icyimage/Shutterstock.com; 92 (tl) © steve estvanik/Shutterstock.com; 92 (tr) © Frans Lanting/National Geographic Creative; 92 (bl) © Elizabeth C. Zurek/Shutterstock.com; 92 (br) © Boris Stroujko/Shutterstock.com; 94 © karrapavan/Shutterstock.com; 96 © Frans Lanting Studio/National Geographic Creative; 97 © Karin Hildebrand Lau/Shutterstock.com; 98 Mircea Costina/Alamy Stock Photo.

Illustrations: 14, 38 David Russell.

Printed at CLDPC, USA, 09-24

Contents

Unit 1 Lessons for life

1a Things they never taught you

Listening eight rules for life

1 ▶ 01 Listen to a talk given to a group of college graduates and answer these questions.

1 What was the speaker going to talk about originally?

_____

_____

2 What does he actually talk about?

_____

_____

flipping burgers (exp) /ˈflɪpɪŋ ˈbɜːrg(ə)z/ a job that involves cooking hamburgers in a fast-food restaurant
entitled (adj) /ɪnˈtaɪt(ə)ld/ believing you deserve to get what you want
nerd (n) *colloquial* /nɜːrd/ a person skilled at something technical but lacking in social skills

2 ▶ 01 Listen again and circle the correct options to complete the rules that the speaker mentions.

1 What you get in life is *just / unjust*.

2 You *must aim for / can't expect* great job conditions from the start.

3 Employers are generally *more strict / less strict* than teachers.

4 Flipping burgers is *not a job you should do / a beginning*.

5 Things will go wrong in your life, and most probably it will be *your / someone else's* fault.

6 The boring chores in life *can be left to others / have to be done by everyone*.

7 In the real world, you will *often / seldom* get a second chance to get things right.

8 Don't underestimate people with good *technical expertise / social skills*.

Grammar time phrases

3 ▶ `01` Complete the sentences with these time phrases. Then listen to the talk again and check your answers.

about 15 years ago	at the time	before that
many years ago	currently	next year
over the last 20 years	rarely	sooner or later

1 _____ , I'm writing a book about scientific inventions.

2 I'm going to give you some rules of life that I read _____ in a book.

3 _____ , I had believed myself to be—as you probably do now—one entitled individual.

4 You will not make $80, 000 _____ .

5 _____ , your grandparents had a different word for burger flipping.

6 But they were like that because _____ they were paying your bills.

7 _____ , schools have abolished the idea of winners and losers.

8 That _____ happens in real life.

9 _____ , you'll end up working for one.

4 Look at the time phrases in these sentences spoken by a student who is about to graduate. Complete the sentences with the correct form of the verbs in parentheses.

1 At the moment, I _____ (take) a break from my studies.

2 Last week, I _____ (attend) a lecture on a career in the diplomatic service.

3 Before that, I _____ (never / be) to a careers advice talk.

4 Nowadays, most graduates _____ (seem) to think that the world owes them a living.

5 I _____ (wonder) for some time what I'm going to do with my life.

6 But I _____ (have to) make a decision in the coming weeks whether to continue studying or apply for a job.

Vocabulary life lessons

5 Complete these sentences. You have been given the first letter of the missing words.

1 My father told me: "Be kind to people and, as much as possible, forgive them when they do wrong. Because in the end, anger and bitterness will just eat you up." He was right, but it's easier s_____ than d_____ .

2 I think the most v_____ lesson anyone has ever taught me came from my English teacher, who said: "Keep an open mind and you will learn a lot."

3 "Do things that take you out of your comfort zone" is a g_____ principle in my life. Because no one progresses by playing it safe.

4 I always make a p_____ of listening to what older people have to say—not just dismissing them as out of touch.

5 I try to learn f_____ my m_____ in life. One thing I've learned is that it's much better to travel light than take loads of stuff with you that you'll never use.

6 I think to remain humble and to try to live as simple a life as possible is a good rule of t_____ .

6 Dictation the problem with advice

▶ `02` Listen to someone describing how advice and wisdom can be misinterpreted. Complete the paragraph.

One _____

_____ .

An example _____

_____ .

One of his main ideas was _____

_____ ,

they will _____ .

He called _____ .

People _____

_____ ,

but _____ ,

_____ .

Unfortunately, _____

_____ ,

which _____ .

1b What's in a name?

Reading **the importance of names**

1 Read the article. Which of these statements (a, b, or c) best represents the author's view?

a Our names should help describe our character.

b Names are useful in giving a person a sense of identity.

c Native American names are useful because they identify social status.

2 Read the article again. Are the sentences true (T) or false (F)?

1 Native Americans share a belief in the significance of names.   T   F

2 It is common for Native Americans to name people after things in the natural world.   T   F

3 Native American names can evolve as people go through life.   T   F

4 Names usually reflect something the parents saw at the time of the child's birth.   T   F

5 Many cultures still use names to indicate the place people were born.   T   F

6 In the West, nicknames are always used to identify someone's social status.   T   F

What's in a name?

Do you feel that your name is an essential part of who you are? What factors did your parents consider when they named you? Had they already been thinking about the name before you were born?

For some, names mean little. For others, such as Native Americans, who have been following the same naming traditions for generations, it is a critical part of one's identity. Although traditions differ from one Native American tribe to another, all tribes attach great importance to the name or names that each individual is given.

You are probably familiar with Native American names taken from nature, such as Laughing Water, Rolling Thunder, White Feather, etc. (NB the belief that such names derive from what their parents were looking at when the child was born is false.) You are probably less aware that their names can also describe certain attributes, such as character (e.g., Independent) or physical appearance (e.g., Broad Shoulders) or social status (e.g., Wife). Among some tribes, these names are continually changing according to people's achievements or life experiences. In some cases, a person will change names three or four times during their life.

Names in Native American culture are descriptive, reminding the bearer of their place in nature or of their reputation in society. In other cultures, surnames often denoted where a person came from or what their family profession was: "Julie London," "James Carpenter" are examples in English. But even if such names still exist, they are no longer an indication of a person's identity.

Perhaps the most similar thing to the Native American tradition in modern Western society is the nickname. My given name is Sarah, but my parents and childhood friends know me as "Sally," a derivative name that has no particular meaning. The people I met at college nicknamed me "Starah" (i.e., "starer") because I have a bad habit of staring at people. Since I have been with my husband, my name has returned to Sarah. Such nicknames may not have the descriptive power of Native American names, but they do serve as important markers of the stages in our lives. Who knows what name people will be calling me in another ten years?

Grammar the continuous aspect

3 Find and name five different continuous tenses used in the article.

4 Look at these pairs of sentences with simple and continuous verb forms. What is the difference in meaning—if any—in the pairs of sentences?

1 a The name Lucas **is** very popular.
   b The name Lucas **is getting** very popular.

2 a People always **pronounce** my name wrong.
   b People **are** always **pronouncing** my name wrong.

3 a They**'ve made** a list of names for their baby, who is due in May.
   b They**'ve been making** a list of names for their baby, who is due in May.

4 a At one time, they **had thought** of giving all their children names beginning with "M."
   b At one time, they **had been thinking** of giving all their children names beginning with "M."

5 a When I **got** married, I decided to change my surname to Romano.
   b When I **was getting** married, I decided to change my surname to Romano.

6 a They've had five boys, so they **hope** the next baby is a girl.
   b They've had five boys, so they**'ll be hoping** the next baby is a girl.

5 Complete these sentences with the correct tense. Use six continuous forms and two simple forms.

1 Sorry I was late picking you up. _____ _____ (you / wait) there long?

2 I can smell cigarettes. _____ (someone / smoke) in here?

3 I heard a scream and ran toward the river. A boy _____ (play) too close to the bank and (fall) _____ in.

4 Sorry I can't meet you later. I'm afraid I _____ (work) late tonight.

5 We _____ (live) in one room for the last three months because builders _____ (repair) our roof.

6 I _____ (hear) a lot of strange stories in my time, but that is probably the strangest.

Vocabulary personality and identity

6 Match the personality types (1–5) with the descriptions (a–e).

1 a control freak   a is very lively and sociable
   ____
2 a driven person   b is independent and does not follow conventions
   ____
3 a family person   c wants to manage every aspect of a situation
   ____
4 a free spirit   d puts home life before other things
   ____
5 the life of the party e is motivated and ambitious
   ____

Wordbuilding binomial pairs

7 Circle the correct options to complete the sentences.

1 Can I have some *quiet and peace / peace and quiet*, please? I'm trying to concentrate.

2 As far as business trips go, it was great— *sweet and short / short and sweet*.

3 That was my first marathon. I have a few *pains and aches / aches and pains* now, but no injuries.

4 *Then and now / Now and then*, I wonder if I should have gone to college.

5 The event is not all *fun and games / games and fun*. There is a serious side to it, too.

6 *First and foremost / Foremost and first*, we choose a name that we hope is not too common.

7 *Large and by / By and large*, it's a pretty good place to live.

8 Pronunciation linking in word pairs

a ▶ 03 Listen to how these binomial word pairs are linked with *and* as a weak form.

1 I hear you **loud and clear**.
2 He'll be **up and about** in no time.
3 It's a game of **cat and mouse**.
4 She's **sick and tired** of people asking what she's going to do with her life.
5 The job has been a bit **up and down** lately.
6 It's **part and parcel** of being a parent.

b Practice saying the sentences in Exercise 8a in the same way.

9 Match the binomial word pairs (1–6) from Exercise 8a with the correct definitions (a–f).

a changeable _____   d clearly _____
b fed up (with) _____   e out of one's sick bed
c an integral element   _____
   _____   f one trying to catch
                              the other _____

1c The English we speak

Listening the evolution of English

1 ▶ 04 Look at these statements about the English language. Do you think the statements are true (T) or false (F)? Then listen to a lecture on the evolution of English, and check your answers.

1 Throughout its history, the English language has been subject to outside influences. T F

2 English is principally a Germanic language. T F

3 The language of Shakespeare is very different from modern English. T F

4 People living in the colonies tried to preserve the integrity of British English. T F

5 Many people around the world speak a very simplified, functional form of English. T F

6 The constant adaptation of English has been a negative thing. T F

2 ▶ 04 Listen again and circle the correct option (a or b) according to the speaker. Pause each time before moving onto the next question.

1 The English language has:
   a influenced other cultures.
   b both influenced and been influenced by other cultures.

2 The fact that Anglo-Saxon, not Latin, was the dominant influence on English is:
   a unlike other countries in Western Europe.
   b because the Romans were hated in Britain.

3 The language stopped changing so fast after the 16th century because:
   a books became more common.
   b no one invaded Britain after that date.

4 The speaker implies that compared to British English, the language used by Americans is:
   a more open. b more refined.

5 The author suggests that English is now a global language because:
   a it is such an adaptable language.
   b it became the language of international trade.

6 Non-native speakers who want to speak English:
   a must choose for themselves what kind of English they want to speak.
   b must be careful not to learn the wrong version of English.

3 Circle the correct definition (a or b) for the words in bold from the lecture.

1 The **legacy** of the Romans is evident in the Romance languages.
   a great achievement b gift to future generations

2 Instead of replacing English, French was **assimilated** into it.
   a incorporated   b transformed

3 The language continued to remain rather **organic**.
   a basic   b in a state of evolution

4 From this point in history, British colonialism **thrived**.
   a did well   b began to diminish

5 English was successful in its global reach because it was a **versatile** language.
   a simple to use   b easy to adapt

Word focus *life*

4 Complete the sentences with *life* using these words.

fact	larger	lifelike
saver	time	walks

1 Jenny is a _____ -**than-life** character; you know when she's in the room!

2 Thanks for covering my shift yesterday. It was a real **life-**_____ .

3 Teaching is a profession that attracts people from **all** _____ **of life**.

4 It's **a** _____ **of life** that you won't get anywhere without effort.

5 That statue of a cat in your backyard is incredibly _____ .

6 My daughter loves college. She**'s having the** _____ **of her life**.

1d How did you get into that?

Real life getting to know people

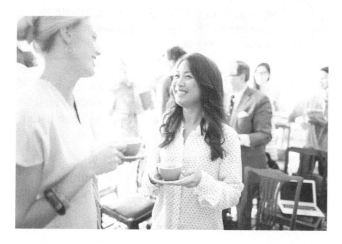

1 ▶ 05 Listen to the conversations. Note down where each conversation takes place and what details you learn about each person.

Conversation 1

Place: _____

Teresa: _____

Ana: _____

Conversation 2

Place: _____

Jeff: _____

Khalid: _____

2 ▶ 05 Complete these questions and statements using ONE word in each space. Then listen to the conversations again and check your answers.

Conversation 1

1 What did you _____ _____ the talk?

2 Sorry, I _____ _____ introduced myself. I'm Teresa.

3 _____ in Spain is it?

4 Do you _____ _____ joining me?

Conversation 2

1 Where are you _____ ?

2 I'm Jeff, _____ the _____ .

3 What are you _____ to be _____ ?

4 Wow, that sounds _____ .

3 What do you think the speakers meant (a or b) when they used the phrases in bold?

1 a lot of **food for thought**
  a things to consider
  b unanswered questions

2 it's **not a million miles from** there
  a not so far from
  b not so different from

3 let me just **get rid of** all these papers
  a throw away
  b find somewhere to put

4 your **best bet** would be …
  a best chance
  b best route

5 **way above my head**, I'm afraid
  a too stressful for me
  b too difficult for me

4 Pronunciation merged words in everyday phrases

a ▶ 06 Listen to the sentences with merged words. Complete the sentences.

1 _____ the exhibition?

2 _____ company is it, exactly?

3 _____ being the only boy in a family of girls?

4 Sorry, _____ that before.

5 _____ the course?

6 So, _____ before?

b Listen again and repeat each sentence.

5 Listen and respond meeting a stranger

▶ 07 You have been invited to dinner by an old friend, Nicola, in a foreign town you are visiting. Someone at the dinner who you don't know comes up to speak to you. Respond with your own words. Then compare your response with the model answer that follows.

> Hi there, I don't think we've met. I'm Antony.

> Hi, Antony. Nice to meet you. I'm José.

1e Company policy

Writing taking notes

1 ▶ 08 Look at these notes that an employee took during a short talk about unpaid leave (i.e., time off work) and sabbaticals (i.e., a long period of leave given every few years in some jobs, e.g., universities). Listen and complete the notes.

> ### Sabbaticals and unpaid leave
>
> • formal document in 2 wks
>
> • sabbaticals, i.e., paid leave: 3 mths for every 6 yrs worked if on ¹ _____ or above; only for full-time staff; part-time staff arrangements TBC
>
> • unpaid leave: ² _____ decides on each case, e.g., sick parents; no unpaid leave for people who have worked for less than ³ _____

2 **Writing skill using abbreviations**

▶ 08 What do you think these abbreviations from the notes mean? Write the words in full. Then listen again and check the words the speaker actually uses.

1 wks _____
2 i.e. _____
3 mths _____
4 yrs _____
5 TBC _____
6 e.g. _____

3 Write abbreviations for these words.

1 approximately _____
2 regarding _____
3 including _____
4 and so on _____
5 ten in the morning _____
6 hours _____
7 please note _____
8 percent _____
9 second _____
10 per week _____

4 Write this message in full sentences.

> Jeff called at 11 a.m. Wants you to go to Atlanta to discuss contract details, i.e. commission, quantities, etc. Time of mtg tbc. NB not in office til Thurs.

5 ▶ 09 You are going to take notes on a talk to company employees about vacation policy. First, look at the guidelines for taking notes. Then listen and complete the notes.

1 Only include important information.
2 Reduce the number of words by omitting articles, auxiliary verbs, unnecessary pronouns.
3 Use abbreviations.

> New policy
> _____
> _____
> _____
> _____
>
> Reasons for policy
> _____
> _____
> _____
>
> Employee responsibilities
> _____
> _____
> _____
> _____
>
> Details
> _____
> _____
> _____
> _____

Wordbuilding binomial pairs

1 Circle the correct word to complete each binomial pair.

1   more *and / or* less
2   take it *and / or* leave it
3   cut *and / but* dried
4   out *and / or* about
5   slowly *and / but* surely
6   live *and / but* learn
7   wear *and / to* tear
8   sink *and / or* swim
9   give *and / but* take

2 Complete these sentences using the pairs in Exercise 1.

1   There's _____ in any relationship. You can't have everything your own way.

2   The sofa looks almost new. There's just a little _____ on the cushion covers.

3   My grandmother's 89 now and _____ stuck at home. She doesn't get _____ as she used to.

4   In my first job, no one showed me what I had to do at all—it was just _____ .

5   The negotiation is pretty _____ , as I see it. I've said what I want and, frankly, they can _____ .

6   We're making progress _____ . It hasn't been an enjoyable experience, but you _____ , I suppose.

Learning skills using idioms

3 Try to answer these questions about idioms.

1   What are the benefits of using idioms in your English?

2   What is the effect on the listener if you get the idiom wrong?

3   Are these statements true (T) or false (F)?

a   Choosing whether to use an idiom or not depends on the context (your audience, whether you're writing or speaking, etc.).   T   F

b   Even if you don't speak the language well, including a few idioms can give a better impression.   T   F

c   Idioms change more quickly than other aspects of the language.   T   F

d   Only use idioms that are new and current.   T   F

e   Idioms and slang are the same thing.   T   F

4 Look at the options in these sentences. Do you think it is appropriate or not to use the idiom in each case?

1 A job interview

A: So tell me a little about yourself, Mr. Barton.
B: Well, I'm 34 years old and *a real go-getter / very ambitious*.

2 A letter advising a friend about investing money in shares

A good *rule of thumb / principle* is always to spread your investments among different sectors.

Check!

5 Take the quiz. All the answers are in Student Book Unit 1.

1 Complete these quotations.

a   "Better to walk without knowing where than to _____ doing nothing."   (Tuareg proverb)

b   "If you want to make peace with your enemy, you have to _____ with your enemy." (Nelson Mandela)

c   "Learn from the mistakes of others. You can't live long enough to make them all _____ ."   (Eleanor Roosevelt)

d   "But love is _____ ."   (Shakespeare)

2 What are the opposites of these types of people? You have been given the first letter.

a   a realist   ≠   a d_____
b   a serious person   ≠   a j_____
c   a shy type   ≠   an o_____ type

3 Rearrange the letters to make time phrases.

a   simple present
    n a y d o w a s   _____
    l e g a r e n l y   _____

b   present continuous
    t a   e h t   o t n e m m   _____

c   present perfect
    o s   f r a   _____
    c l e r e n t y   _____

d   past perfect
    p u   t o   h e n t   _____

Unit 2 More than a job

2a Golden worm diggers

Listening *yartsa gunbu*

1 ▶10 Look at the photo and then listen to a news report. Answer the questions.

   1 Where are these people?

      _____

   2 What are the people looking for, and why?

      _____

   3 What would they normally be doing for a living?

      _____

2 ▶10 Read this summary. Then listen again and complete the summary using one word in each blank.

In May and June, on the Tibetan Plateau, you can see people [1] _____ the grass for a small fungus called *yartsa gunbu*. *Yartsa gunbu* is highly valued for its [2] _____ properties. It grows inside the body of a [3] _____ and then sends a small [4] _____ above the ground. People who [5] _____ it believe it improves your life [6] _____, and so demand for it has [7] _____ in recent years. The local people, who in the past made a living by herding yaks and sheep, now make much more money from *yartsa gunbu*. But [8] _____ are worried about the [9] _____ of *yartsa gunbu* and think it may die out.

Wordbuilding **phrasal verb** *get*

3 Circle the correct option.

   1 I'm the only one in the family earning any money at the moment, but we *get by / get through*.

   2 I'm really not in the mood for a party, but I can't *get away with / get out of* it. I promised Sheree I'd go.

   3 Well, thanks for all your advice. I'll *get back to / get through to* you if I need anything else.

   4 I think Jake will go a long way. He's very positive. If he has a disappointment, he *gets over / gets around* it very quickly.

   5 I wish she had said what was on her mind. I couldn't understand what she was *getting at / getting to*.

   6 I'm sorry I haven't fixed the latch on the window yet. I'll try to *get around to / get away with* it later today.

   7 He's constantly stretching the truth and no one ever says anything to him. How can he *get away with it / get over it*?

Grammar perfect forms

4 ▶ **10** Look at these sentences from the report. Which verb did the speaker use? Listen to the report again and check your answers.

1 It's as if someone *had dropped / had been dropping* a valuable ring and then asked their friends to help search for it.

2 What they *have looked for / are looking for* is a small fungus called *yartsa gunbu*.

3 It's so prized in China that half a kilo *was known / has been known* to sell for up to $50,000.

4 One couple I talked to *had been searching / had searched* all day and *has found / found* only thirty specimens.

5 Zhaxicaiji *has started / started* her own *yartsa* company in 1998.

6 Since then, the business *has grown / grew* year after year.

7 The cycle will stop, because the fungus that infects the larvae *will be disappearing / will have disappeared.*

8 Perhaps the next generation of golden worm diggers *will be searching / will have searched* harder than ever.

5 Complete these sentences by putting the verbs in the correct tense. Use simple or perfect forms.

Does *yartsa gunbu* actually work? Recent research
[1] _____ (show) that it helps the blood absorb more oxygen, which in turn
[2] _____ (help) the user to feel more energetic.

People in the West [3] _____ (criticize) the use of herbs in Chinese medicine for being unscientific, but in fact, it is a practice that
[4] _____ (be based) on thousands of years of practice. Moreover, many of the ingredients are the same as those in Western medicines. A US study in 2002 [5] _____ (show) that in nearly 50 percent of the new drugs produced in the previous twenty years, scientists
[6] _____ (use) natural plants as a starting point.

So far, Western medicine [7] _____ (not / exploit) Chinese knowledge of herbs. One drug, however, that [8] _____ (be) very successful in treating malaria comes from the plant artemisinin. But there is no sign that more drugs like this [9] _____ (be developed) any time soon. This is a shame as, without a doubt, there [10] _____ (be) a lot that the West can learn from Chinese medicine.

Vocabulary work and life

6 Complete these sentences. You have been given the first letter of the missing words.

1 The animals are our l_____ . Without them, we couldn't survive.

2 When we interview new applicants, we always give them a simple t_____ to perform.

3 Some students go on to college, but many opt to learn a t_____ like plumbing.

4 Medicine is more than just a job; it's a v_____ .

5 It's difficult to make a decent l_____ as an artist, unless you become very well known.

7 Pronunciation extra /ɪ/, /iː/, or /aɪ/

▶ **11** Look at the underlined syllables in these words and put the words into categories according to the vowel sound each contains: /ɪ/ as in *bit*, /iː/ as in *beat*, or /aɪ/ as in *bite*. Then listen and check your answers.

me<u>di</u>cinal	sur<u>vive</u>	spe<u>ci</u>fic	<u>ti</u>ny	<u>fi</u>nancial
<u>pri</u>vate	<u>pre</u>vious	pre<u>scribe</u>	<u>vi</u>sa	re<u>vi</u>talize
un<u>sci</u>entific	spe<u>ci</u>men	cater<u>pi</u>llar	<u>ki</u>lo	ar<u>tist</u>

8 Dictation interview with a journalist

▶ **12** Listen to an interview with the journalist who reported the story of the golden worm diggers. Complete his answers.

I: So, John, how did you come across this story?

J: [1] I _____
_____ .

I: And what was it that interested you this time?

J: [2] Well, _____
_____
_____ .

I: And what was that in this case?

J: [3] I _____
_____
_____ .

2b Deep-sea line fishers

Reading a game of cat and mouse

1 Read the article about an expedition to catch a bluefin tuna. Answer the questions.

1 What is difficult about catching these fish?

_____

2 What method do the people in the article use?

_____

line (n) /laɪn/
bait (n) /beɪt/
rod (n) /rɒd/
reel (n) /riːl/
hook (n) /hʊk/

rod
hook
reel
line
bait

2 Read the article again. Are these sentences true (T) or false (F)? Or is there not enough information (N) to say if the sentences are true or false?

1	The narrator is new to sea fishing.	T	F	N
2	If the fish weren't so heavy, they'd be easy to catch.	T	F	N
3	Numbers of bluefin tuna have declined because of the high number of line fishers.	T	F	N
4	Bluefin tuna generally feed on other smaller fish.	T	F	N
5	Troy used his instinct to know where the fish were.	T	F	N
6	It's necessary to leave the line a little loose to make the fish think you are not interested.	T	F	N

Deep-sea line fishers

Some people have compared catching a bluefin tuna to trying to catch a car going at eighty kilometers per hour. So, not having done any line fishing at sea before, I was pretty apprehensive—but also excited—about the trip that my friend, a professional line fisher named Troy had organized.

At the same time, my hopes were not high. Ninety-five percent of the time, bluefin tuna line fishers come back empty-handed and a few hundred dollars worse off in the attempt. Just finding the fish is difficult enough, but once you've found them, you are then faced with the task of landing a fish that can weigh in excess of 300 kilos.

Of course, tracking them down has become more difficult in recent years because of overfishing. Because demand for tuna is so high, fishing companies employ an intensive form of fishing called "purse seine," where they use big circular nets to trap the tuna. This has devastated the Atlantic tuna population, reducing it by over eighty percent in the last thirty years.

Three days before we were due to set off, Troy got a call from a friend who informed him of a secret fishing spot about sixty kilometers off the coast. Since we had nothing else to do, we headed there that evening, and the following morning, just as he had said, thousands of bluefin tuna showed up.

In order to keep our prey interested, we dropped chunks of fish into the water and then baited our lines and let them out. Tuna feed at depths of fifty to a hundred meters, so you need a lot of line. For about two hours, we sat there waiting for something to happen, and then suddenly Troy's rod bent dramatically and the reel started spinning furiously, casting line out at an incredible rate.

Knowing the fish like to swim toward the boat to make you think they are off the line, Troy jumped on the rod so that he could keep the line tight. Then we followed the fish, steering the boat in the same direction, while Troy slowly reeled it in. After about an hour of this, the fish started to get tired of us chasing it and it came closer to the surface, where we could see it. "Grab the harpoon gun," Troy shouted and I knew that my moment had come.

Idioms safety

3 Match the two parts to make idioms connected with safety.

1. second _____   a side
2. cut _____   b the book
3. be on the safe _____   c side of caution
4. follow _____   d nature
5. do things by _____   e corners
6. better to be safe _____   f than sorry
7. err on the _____   g the correct procedure

4 Complete these sentences using idioms from Exercise 3.

1. I always wear a bicycle helmet, even if I'm riding a short distance—just to _____ .

2. I felt a little embarrassed wearing a helmet, elbow pads, and knee pads when I went roller-blading, but I thought it's _____ .

3. Safety is actually _____ to me because I used to have a job repairing electrical lines.

4. It's very tempting to _____ when you think you can do something more quickly by not observing all the safety rules.

5. If you _____ rather than thinking you know better, you will be fine.

Grammar passive forms

5 Rewrite the sentences transforming one verb in each sentence to make a passive construction.

1. My friend Troy had organized the trip.

   _____

2. Once you've found the fish, that's only the beginning of your task.

   _____

3. In "purse seine" fishing, people use big circular nets to trap the tuna.

   _____

4. Purse seine fishing has devastated the Atlantic tuna population in the last thirty years.

   _____

5. Troy jumped on the rod so that he could keep the line tight.

   _____

6. The fish started to get tired of us chasing it.

   _____

6 Complete these sentences with passive constructions using the verbs in parentheses. Use *be* or *get* to form each passive verb as you think appropriate.

1. Did you hear about poor Esty? She _____ (call) in to work over the weekend—on her birthday!

2. I wish they would just let me get on with the job. I'm tired of _____ (tell) what to do.

3. Please be careful using that ax. You _____ (injure).

4. I don't mind driving, but it's more relaxing _____ (drive)—depending on who the driver is, of course!

5. I submit my photos to the newspaper, but if they don't like them, I _____ (not / pay).

6. _____ (you / invite) to the opening of the exhibition? It's next Friday.

7 Read the passage and underline the best options (active or passive) to complete the text. Where you think either could work, underline both.

If you had to say what the most dangerous professions in the world are, probably [1]*you would not include fishing / fishing would not be included* on your list. Yet, statistically, deep-sea fishing is the world's riskiest job. In the U.K., fishers have a one in twenty chance of [2]*fishing killing them / being killed* during their working lives. When you consider the conditions that [3]*fishing forces them / they are forced* to work in, it is not surprising: rough seas, freezing temperatures, long hours, and lots of heavy, moving equipment. Another industry that has a similarly high injury rate is logging (cutting down trees for wood). [4]*Loggers also work long hours / Long hours are also worked by loggers* and they, too, use heavy, dangerous equipment. They are also at risk of injury from heavy tree trunks slipping or falling. One job that might have been on your list is mining. Although [5]*they employ fewer people / fewer people are employed* in mines these days, it remains a dangerous profession. This is not just because of the obvious risks of mines collapsing, but also because of the long-term effects of [6]*breathing in poor air / poor air being breathed in*.

2c Guerrilla geographer

Listening Daniel Raven-Ellison

1 ▶ 13 Listen to part of a radio program about Daniel Raven-Ellison's new approach to geography. Which of these statements (a, b, or c) best summarizes this new approach?

a a critical approach that challenges people to question traditional geography teaching

b an inclusive approach that encourages communities to redesign their neighborhoods

c a practical and fun approach that promotes social and environmental awareness

2 ▶ 13 Listen again and complete these statements and questions.

1 What was Daniel Raven-Ellison's job before?
_____

2 For Raven-Ellison, geography is more than just
_____ .

3 What kind of exploration does he want to promote among children? _____

4 Guerrilla geography is all about having
_____ .

5 He says most city guides are selective in what they show, but his movies show the
_____ .

6 What is the best way to appreciate your neighborhood properly?
_____

7 The fun nature of *Mission: Explore*'s tasks disguise the fact that you need to use
_____ .

8 For Raven-Ellison, education should encourage people to be _____ .

3 Look at the words in bold from the program. Circle the correct synonym (a or b).

1 Outdoor exploration **spurs** innovative problem solving …
   a encourages   b involves

2 Walking gives you a different, more **tangible** perspective …
   a enjoyable   b real

3 It's a **hands-on** format that's very accessible.
   a lively   b practical

4 … moments that will be **crucial** to tackling issues like climate change …
   a essential   b helpful

Word focus *foot/feet*

4 Match the idioms (1–4) with their definitions (a–d).

1 I **got off on the wrong foot** with my boss when I told him I didn't like using computers. _____

2 He offered to give the talk with me, but then at the last minute, he **got cold feet**. _____

3 The company **shot itself in the foot** by not investing in new technology when it had the chance. _____

4 Don't worry if it all seems strange at first. You'll soon **find your feet**. _____

a have a bad start

b start to feel more confident in a new situation

c withdraw from doing something because you feel anxious

d do something that damages your own situation or prospects

5 The idioms in bold are in the wrong sentences. Replace the idioms with the correct ones and make changes as needed.

1 She **shot herself in the foot,** but relations with her colleagues are much better now.

2 I hope I didn't **have two left feet** when I told her how like her sister she was.

3 I've never been good at dancing—I **get off on the wrong foot**.

4 She really **followed in her father's footsteps** by not taking the promotion when she was offered it.

5 People often ask me why I didn't **get my foot in the door** and become a doctor like him.

6 I'm now working for Google. I was very lucky to **put my foot in it** because so many people want to work there.

2d Presenting yourself

Vocabulary personal qualities

1 Look at the statements and write the adjective that sums up this quality. You have been given the first letter.

My strengths? Well, ...

1	I care about doing a good job.	c_____
2	I will always get the job done.	r_____
3	I love my work.	e'_____
4	I want to do well.	m_____
5	I don't get distracted from my work.	f_____
6	I'm willing to do anything I'm asked to do.	f_____
7	I keep things in order so as to be efficient.	w_____-o_____
8	If I don't have the tools to do something, I'll find another way.	r_____

Real life presenting yourself

2 ▶ 14 Listen to a man, Hiroki, presenting himself at an interview for a graduate training program. Answer the questions.

1 What kind of work does the company do?

_____

2 What relevant experience does Hiroki have?

_____

_____

3 ▶ 14 Listen again. Write the five qualities from the list in Exercise 1 that you think Hiroki possesses. Give reasons for your answers.

1 c_____

Reason: _____

2 w_____-o_____

Reason: _____

3 r_____

Reason: _____

4 e_____ and m_____

Reason: _____

4 Pronunciation word stress

▶ 15 Look at these words used in the interview and underline the stressed syllable(s) in each word. Then listen, check, and practice.

1	experience	4	relevant
2	infrastructure	5	authorities
3	particular	6	suitability

5 Listen and respond a suitable candidate

▶ 16 You are at an interview for a job working as a trainee hotel manager at a top San Francisco hotel. The interviewer asks you some questions. Respond with your own words. Then compare your response with the model answer that follows.

1

So can you tell me a little about yourself and what attracted you to this job?

Yes, my name is Eduardo Torres, and I'm a graduate in hotel management. I have been working for the last year at a small hotel in the country, and I'd like to get a job with a bigger hotel.

2e A letter of application

Writing a cover letter or email

1 Writing skill fixed expressions

a Complete these phrases from a cover letter. You have been given the first letter of the missing words.

a The job a_____ me because I know of your company's reputation for …

b I am a_____ for an interview any time.

c I am writing in r_____ to your advertisement for …

d C_____ , I am working for …

e A_____ someone who has worked in this field previously, I think I am a s_____ candidate.

f Please find a_____ my resume.

g Thank you for t_____ the time to c_____ this application.

h Regarding the specific r_____ you mention, I also have: …

b Look at the key elements of a cover letter and match 1–8 with the phrases (a–h) from Exercise 1a.

1 State the job applied for and where and when it was advertised. _____

2 Refer to your resume. _____

3 Mention your present situation. _____

4 Explain why you are suited to the job. _____

5 Show that you know something about their organization. _____

6 Respond to any key qualifications you have that are needed for this job. _____

7 Thank them for their time. _____

8 Explain where and when you can be contacted. _____

2 Read the cover letter. Which of the key elements (1–8) from Exercise 1b are missing?

Dear Ms. Newman:

I am writing in response to your advertisement on the Jobsonline website for a fundraiser at Harmon College. I am enclosing my resume, which details my qualifications and relevant experience.

The job attracted me because I know several people who have studied at Harmon College and I am aware of the good work that you do in helping the long-term unemployed get retrained to enter the world of work again.

Regarding the specific requirements that you mention:

· I have a Master's degree in economics.

· I am a resident in the Philadelphia area.

· I have my own car.

I am available for an interview at any time, given reasonable notice. Many thanks for considering this application.

I look forward to hearing from you.

Yours sincerely,

Jane Knowles

Jane Knowles

3 Write extra text for each missing element. Use your own or invented information. Mark on the letter in Exercise 2 where the extra text should go.

_____

_____

_____

_____

_____

_____

_____

_____

_____

_____

_____

_____

Wordbuilding *get*

1 The verb *get* has multiple meanings (when used alone as well as in phrasal verbs). Try to guess what *get* means in these sentences. (Note that the last two are phrasal verbs.)

1   Sorry, I just don't *get* what you're trying to say. _____

2   Don't *get* too excited about it. It's not certain yet that we'll move to Canada. _____

3   I'm going to try to *get* some time off work next week so that I can review for my exams. _____

4   Put your wallet away. I'll *get* this. _____

5   I'll try to *get* her to change her mind, but I'm not optimistic. _____

6   Don't worry about giving me a ride. I can easily *get* the bus. _____

7   It really *gets to* me that he can make jokes about other people, but he can't take a joke himself. _____

8   To *get ahead* in this profession, you have to keep constantly up to date with new technology. _____

2 Match the meanings (a–h) with the verb *get* in 1–8 in Exercise 1.

a   pay for   e   obtain or be given

b   progress   f   annoy

c   go (on/in)   g   make or persuade

d   understand   h   become

Learning skills listening: top-down strategies

3 Before listening to an excerpt in English, try to use the same strategies that help you understand content when listening in your own language. Ask yourself these questions.

1   What is the context for this listening (an everyday conversation, a lecture, a scientific report, an interview, etc.)?

2   What is the probable attitude of the speaker (e.g., are they trying to persuade/inform/complain, etc.)?

3   Am I listening just for gist or for some specific information (dates, times, names, etc.)?

4   What do I already know about this subject/situation, and what questions would I like to have answered by what I am about to hear?

4 Look at these contexts (1 and 2). Ask yourself questions 2–4 from Exercise 3. Decide a) the probable attitude of the speaker; b) whether you are listening for gist or specific information; and c) what questions you want answered.

1   an interview with a sociologist about her new book on attitudes toward childhood

a   _____

b   _____

c   _____

2   a discussion among three friends about a recently released movie

a   _____

b   _____

c   _____

Check!

5 Take this quiz. All the answers are in Student's Book Unit 2.

1 Complete the descriptions of these people.

a   Kazakh _____

b   M_____ people

c   s_____

2 Look at the attributes (a–c) of each person in Exercise 1 and say what each enables them to do.

a   great patience

b   extraordinary vision

c   being the right weight

3 Complete these grammar explanations.

a   Perfect forms are used to look _____ at an event that has an impact on a _____ time.

b   We sometimes use _____ + past participle, rather than *be* + past participle, to form the passive.

4 Complete the sentences. Then rearrange the first letters of each word to make the name of a character in this unit.

a   Please do _____ hesitate to _____ me if you have any questions.

b   Oh, dear! I hope I didn't put _____ foot _____ it.

c   _____ look forward to _____ from _____ soon.

d   Female smokejumpers do the same _____ as _____ smokejumpers.

Name: J_____ C_____

Unit 3 Design for life

3a My town

Listening my town

1 ▶ 17 You will hear two people talking about towns they live or have lived in. Listen and complete the chart. If no information is given, write NM (not mentioned).

	Glastonbury	Ghent
Location		
Size of town		
Type of town		
Reasons for liking		

2 ▶ 17 Listen again and circle the correct option (a, b, or c) to complete each statement.

1 Glastonbury Festival takes place:
   a in the town of Glastonbury.
   b in some fields near Glastonbury.
   c at a world heritage site.

2 Glastonbury town changed when:
   a some festival-goers began to settle there.
   b the first festival was held in 1970.
   c people realized what a magical place it was.

3 Now the town has an unusual mixture of:
   a ethnic groups.
   b people with different lifestyles.
   c commercial activities.

4 The speaker suggests that not many people visit Ghent because:
   a it's a long way from Brussels and Bruges.
   b they don't know how attractive it is.
   c they think it's just a small provincial town.

5 Ghent is home to a lot of _____ industries.
   a traditional   b shipping   c large

6 The variety of activities in Ghent means that people are quite _____ .
   a tolerant   b educated   c socially active

3 Look at these expressions used by the speakers. Match the words in bold in 1–8 with their definitions (a–h).

1 pleasant **period** houses _____
2 a **transformative** experience _____
3 an **alternative** lifestyle _____
4 it's all a bit **wacky** _____
5 my **adopted** town for a while _____
6 part of its **charm** _____
7 around the old **docks** _____
8 The other **drawback** _____

a life-changing
b attraction
c disadvantage
d unconventional
e area where ships are loaded
f strange and funny
g belonging to a past time
h that you have chosen to live in

Vocabulary describing towns

4 Complete the definitions. You have been given the first two letters of the missing words.

1 A town that is deserted is a gh_____ town.
2 A town that is pleasantly old-fashioned is qu_____ .
3 An area of very poor housing on the edge of a city is called a sh_____town.
4 A part of a city that grows without any planning we call a sp_____ suburb.
5 Another word for *untidy* is me_____ .
6 Buildings that are boring and unimaginatively designed are ch_____ .
7 A town where very little ever happens we call a sl_____ town.
8 Another word for a vacation town by the sea is a seaside re_____ .

Grammar qualifiers

5 ▶ 17 Look at these sentences from the descriptions you heard. Underline the most appropriate form. Then listen again and check your answers.

1 Glastonbury is *fairly / rather* well known around the world for its music festival.
2 All in all, it was *a bit sleepy / quite a sleepy,* traditional kind of English town.
3 Well, now the town is a *quite / rather* odd mix of older, more conservative residents and younger people.
4 But actually, I *like it quite / quite like it*!
5 Actually, it might be *cheating slightly / rather cheating* to call it a town.
6 One of the benefits of having that kind of mix is that people tend to be *a little / quite* open-minded.
7 There's also lots to do, but going out isn't *particularly / rather* cheap.
8 The other drawback is the weather, which is *a bit / pretty* terrible most of the time—gray and rainy.
9 I'm from Italy, and I have to say, it got me down *a bit / fairly* at times.

6 Complete this conversation using an appropriate qualifier in each space.

A: Where did you grow up?
B: Not ¹_____ far from here, actually. In Bourneville.

A: Where's that? I'm not ²_____ familiar with this area.
B: It's ³_____ near the center of Birmingham. I suppose you'd call it a suburb.
A: So what was that like? I imagine it was still ⁴_____ an urban area, wasn't it?
B: Well, no, actually. Bourneville is a very pleasant, leafy kind of suburb. It's got a ⁵_____ interesting history, in fact.
A: In what way?
B: Well, it was specially designed as a model village for workers at the chocolate factory to live in. You know, to keep them happy and productive. And it really is ⁶_____ a special place to live.

7 Pronunciation *quite, fairly,* and *pretty*

▶ 18 Listen to the conversations. For which items does speaker B mean "… but probably not enough"?

1 A: Are you warm?
 B: Mmm. I'm quite warm.
2 A: Are you feeling optimistic?
 B: Hmm … pretty hopeful.
3 A: How was the movie?
 B: I quite liked it.
4 A: Is he interested in the job?
 B: Mmm. He's pretty interested, I think.
5 A: Is it safe?
 B: It's fairly safe.

8 Dictation *talking about places*

▶ 19 Listen to a conversation about a visit to Russia. Complete the conversation.

A: How was your trip to Russia?
B: Great, thanks. We _____ , but _____ .
 We started _____
 Red Square. _____
 the subway. Each _____ .
 The _____ .
A: And how did it compare to St. Petersburg?
B: Very different. St. Petersburg _____ .
 Actually, it _____
 _____ ,
 _____ Moscow _____
 _____ . But _____ .
 You _____ there.

3b Sky caves of Nepal

Reading mysterious dwellings

1 Look at the photo of some unusual caves. Then read the excerpt from an article about the caves and answer the questions.

1 What do you learn about the geography and climate of this area?

_____

_____

2 How many caves are there like the ones in the photo?

_____

3 Why was this place important historically?

_____

4 What was found in the caves?

_____

5 What was the function of the earliest caves?

_____

6 Why did people choose to live in them?

_____

Sky caves of Nepal

Mustang, a former kingdom in northcentral Nepal, is home to one of the world's great archeological finds. In this [1] incredibly inhospitable, wind-savaged place, hidden within the Himalayas, there are an extraordinary number of human-built caves.

Some sit [2] completely by themselves, a single open mouth on a vast face of weathered rock. Others are in groups, occasionally stacked eight or nine floors high, making a sort of vertical neighborhood. Some were dug into the cliffside; others were tunneled from above. Many are thousands of years old. The total number of caves in Mustang, conservatively estimated, is 10,000. Why anyone would choose to build rooms that are [3] extremely difficult and dangerous to access has remained a mystery, and the evidence that might supply an answer has been almost [4] totally erased.

We know that 700 years ago, Mustang was a bustling place: a center of scholarship and art, and a key place on the salt trade route from Tibet to India. Salt was then an [5] extremely valuable commodity. Later, when cheaper salt became available in India, an economic decline set in. Soon the region was all but forgotten, lost beyond the great mountains.

Pete Athans first noticed the caves of Mustang while trekking in 1981. Many appear impossible to reach unless you are a bird, and Athans, a [6] very accomplished mountaineer, was stirred by the challenge they presented.

Over a twelve-year period, Athans made several visits. Most of the caves he looked into were

empty, though they showed signs of domestic habitation. But in others the treasures he and his team found were [7] quite stunning. In one cave they discovered a 26-foot-long mural, in another 8,000 calligraphed manuscripts. Many caves seemed to be elaborate tombs full of [8] absolutely amazing riches.

Evidence now shows that the caves divide into three general periods. Three thousand years ago, they were used as burial chambers. About 1,000 years ago, they became primarily living quarters. Because the territory was frequently fought over, people took refuge in them, placing safety over convenience. After A.D. 1400, when most people had moved to traditional villages, the caves continued to be used—as meditation chambers, military lookouts, or storage units. Some remained as homes, and even today a few families live in them.

Grammar intensifying adverbs

2 Look at the intensifying adverbs in the article. Then circle the adverb that could best replace each adverb in the article.

1 absolutely / extremely
2 entirely / extremely
3 completely / incredibly
4 absolutely / completely
5 absolutely / very
6 extremely / utterly
7 mildly / very
8 vaguely / quite

3 Complete the exchanges about the sky caves story with these intensifying adverbs. There is sometimes more than one possibility.

absolutely	completely	incredibly	quite
really	totally	very	

A: You must have to be a(n) ¹ _____ skilled climber to get into these caves.

B: Yes, you have to be ² _____ fearless.

C: I find it ³ _____ incredible that people could have lived in these caves.

D: I know. It must have been ⁴ _____ difficult to get provisions like food and water up to them.

E: I would ⁵ _____ love to be involved in this kind of work.

F: Yes. It must be ⁶ _____ exciting to discover what's inside the caves.

G: The entrances to some of the burial caves were ⁷ _____ sealed with large boulders.

H: Yes, that's right. The climbers had to ⁸ _____ literally risk their lives to open them up.

4 Pronunciation stress in intensifying adverbs

a ▶ 20 Listen to these sentences with intensifiers and underline the stressed syllables.

1 I'm utterly exhausted.
2 I'd really appreciate that.
3 It's so hot today.
4 It's OK. I quite understand.
5 You're absolutely right.
6 It's very difficult to say.

b Practice saying the sentences with the same stress.

Vocabulary adverb and adjective collocations

5 Match the adverbs (1–9) with the adjectives (a–i) to make collocations. More than one answer may be possible.

1 deadly _____		a	amused
2 ideally _____		b	familiar
3 hopelessly _____		c	optimistic
4 mildly _____		d	reasonable
5 painfully _____		e	serious
6 perfectly _____		f	slow
7 closely _____		g	in love
8 vaguely _____		h	suited
9 wildly _____		i	associated with

6 Complete the sentences with collocations from Exercise 5.

1 I think your estimate that ninety percent of the people will say "yes" is _____ . It'll be more like forty percent.

2 His name sounds _____ to me. I think maybe I met him at a party about three years ago.

3 The review described the play as "laugh out loud funny," but I was only _____ .

4 Even if you bought the suitcase three years ago, it's _____ to ask for a refund if it has a five-year guarantee.

5 I thought she was joking when she said she was going to run the Boston Marathon, but she was _____ .

6 I wish he would get to the point sooner. I find his explanations _____ .

Vocabulary features in a home

7 Look at these features in a home. Are they for storage (S), health and fitness (H), enjoying the sun (E), leisure (L), or convenience (C)?

1 a game room _____
2 a home theater _____
3 a library _____
4 a walk-in closet _____
5 An en suite bathroom _____
6 a garage _____
7 a state-of-the-art kitchen _____
8 a roof garden _____
9 a gym _____
10 a sauna _____

3c Biomimetic architecture

Listening the influence of nature

1 ▶ 21 Look at the photos and captions. Then listen to an interview with an architectural historian about "biomimetics." Answer the questions.

1 What does *biomimetics* mean?

_____

2 How do the three structures in the photos relate to biomimetics?

_____

2 ▶ 21 Listen again and circle the correct option (a, b, or c). Pause each time before moving onto the next question.

1 According to the historian, the term *biomimetics*:
   a is relatively recent.
   b is an old term.
   c can be applied to anything that copies nature.

2 The examples of new materials she gives are materials that copy:
   a water-based animals.
   b animals in general.
   c animals and plants.

3 When designing the Sagrada Familia, Gaudí took inspiration from:
   a models he had made.
   b nature's forms.
   c the human body.

4 The design of the Sagrada Familia:
   a confused the public.
   b divided public opinion.
   c brought Gaudí great fame.

5 There are a lot of biomimetic buildings now that are:
   a named after animals.
   b known by the name of something in the natural world.
   c given nicknames by their creators.

6 The Eastgate Centre in Harare uses biomimetics to avoid:
   a becoming too cold.
   b looking like a conventional office and shopping complex.
   c having to be cooled artificially.

Sagrada Familia, Barcelona

Swiss Re Tower, London

A termite mound

3 Match these words in bold from the interview with the correct definition (a or b).

1 … the term *biomimetics*, which was **coined** in the 1950s …
   a first created   b made popular

2 … high-tech swimsuits that **replicate** shark skin.
   a use   b imitate

3 … he created a very **organic**-looking building …
   a simple   b natural

4 … one of the most **hideous** buildings in the world.
   a beautiful   b ugly

Word focus *ground*

4 Complete these sentences to make idioms with *ground*.

1 You shouldn't give in to pressure just because it comes from people who have more experience. _____ **your ground**.

2 She refused to comment on the situation **on the** _____ **that** it was a private matter.

3 Using the latest laser technology, they are **breaking** _____ **ground** _____ medical surgery.

4 He has some great ideas, but that's all they are: ideas. Because none of them ever _____ _____ **the ground**.

5 Thanks—that was really productive. I'm amazed that we _____ **so much ground** in just an hour.

3d A lot going for it

Real life expressing opinions

1 ▶ 22 Listen to part of a discussion about a proposal to put a new coffee lounge into a large open-plan office, which is on the 14th floor of an office building. Write down two of the arguments mentioned in favor of the proposal and one against it.

For

_____

_____

Against

_____

_____

2 ▶ 22 Complete the phrases used by the speakers to express their opinions. Then listen again and check your answers.

1   First of _____ , I should say that I think it's _____ a good idea.
2   It has a lot of things to _____ it.
3   But I _____ _____ say there's a risk in that.
4   I kind of _____ _____ that. The thing about an open-plan office is ...
5   The informal chats are something we _____ _____ the importance of.
6   So I'm very _____ in _____ of this proposal, particularly _____ that we are all working in ...
7   Oh, and _____ the _____ , including a screen with industry news on it in the room is a nice _____ .

3 Pronunciation linking vowel sounds (intrusion)

a ▶ 23 Listen to these phrases and write the sound or letter that links *and* to the word before it.

1   food and water _____
2   tea and cookies _____
3   wait and see _____
4   go and ask _____
5   you and me _____

b ▶ 24 Look at these phrases and mark the words that are linked. If an extra sound (/w/ or /j/) is needed, write this too. Then listen and check your answers.

E.g.   every so often
                    w

1   first of all
2   with a bit of luck
3   as far as I'm aware
4   between you and me
5   at the end of the day
6   I have no idea, I'm afraid

c   Practice saying the phrases in the same way.

4 Listen and respond giving your opinion

▶ 25 Someone is going to ask your opinions on where we choose to live and the importance of our surroundings. Respond with your own words. Then compare your response with the model answer that follows.

1

> *Would you prefer to have a large living space or somewhere that's small and cozy?*

> *Personally, I'd like to have a lot of space, but maybe that seems a bit selfish.*

3e High-rise living

Writing an opinion essay

1 Look at the elements of an opinion essay (1–4). Then read the two paragraphs (a and b) from an opinion essay about whether it is good for people to live in high-rise buildings. Which elements do the paragraphs represent?

1 analyze the question and set out your starting point
2 give your opinion and present the arguments supporting it
3 deal with opposing arguments
4 make your conclusion

a So, as with so many things, in the end we must balance the advantages and disadvantages and then make a choice. For me, even though there are great benefits of high-rise buildings, these benefits are outweighed by the cost to human interaction. After all, what use is a pleasant environment if most of the time you are isolated from other people in a small apartment seventy meters from the ground? _____

b The pressure for space in our cities has demanded that we build upward, with taller and taller buildings, rather than build outward. It is true that it is not particularly desirable to keep expanding our cities outward into green, undeveloped land outside the city limits, but there are other solutions to providing more homes, such as the creation of compact living spaces. Some high-rise buildings could still be retained for non-residential activity, for example, as offices. _____

2 Do you think the writer is for or against high-rise living? What arguments does he/she concede to the other side?

_____
_____
_____

3 Writing skill discourse markers

Match the two halves of each comment about city life.

1 Living in an apartment downtown is a bit noisy. _____
2 Even though we live twenty floors up, _____
3 It feels very nice to live in an old house. _____
4 Our building is not the tallest in the neighborhood. _____
5 Most of the apartments are rented by companies for their employees. _____
6 We wanted to be somewhere with a sense of community, _____

a After all, very few individuals could afford to rent privately.
b Having said that, it is extremely convenient.
c that is to say, a place where people enjoy interacting.
d Admittedly, the maintenance costs are higher.
e our view of the city is blocked by other tall buildings.
f Indeed, there are some buildings over sixty floors high.

4 Write your own answer to the question: *Is it good for people to live in high-rise buildings?* Follow the structure suggested in Exercise 1. You can use ideas from those two paragraphs if you wish.

Wordbuilding renting an apartment

1 Use these words to complete the conversation between a student looking for an apartment and a real estate agent.

advance	bills	budget	commission
deposit	furnished	landlord	move
properties	references	rent	rentals
share	studio	tenant	

S: Hi, I'm looking to ¹ _____ a small apartment, like a ² _____ apartment, for three months. Do you do short-term ³ _____ ?

A: Yes, but only for ⁴ _____ apartments. Is it just for you, or are you planning to ⁵ _____ ? And when is this from?

S: Just me and I'm hoping to ⁶ _____ in as soon as possible.

A: OK. And what's your ⁷ _____ ?

S: Well, including the ⁸ _____ , no more than $900 a month.

A: OK. I think we have a few ⁹ _____ that will interest you. You just need to know that we don't take any ¹⁰ _____ from you, the ¹¹ _____ , just from the ¹² _____ , who has to pay us a small fee. But you will need to pay a ¹³ _____ of one month's rent and one month's rent in ¹⁴ _____ . And you'll also need to provide some ¹⁵ _____ , including one from your employer.

Learning skills listening: bottom-up strategies

2 When you listen to fast native speech, you may be faced with the difficulty of decoding the sounds you hear. Look at this list of key things to recognize in native speech.

1 being able to recognize a word from its stressed syllable

2 understanding the place of weak forms (auxiliary verbs, prepositions, articles) in a sentence

3 understanding linking so that you can separate the words that have been linked

4 picking out the key word in a sentence (the one that carries the main meaning)

3 ▶ 26 Look at the stressed syllables in the words in this sentence. Then listen to the sentence.

The de<u>vel</u>opment of <u>en</u>ergy-ef<u>fic</u>ient <u>homes</u> has <u>changed</u> the way <u>houses</u> are <u>built</u>.

4 ▶ 27 Underline the stressed syllables in the words in these sentences. Then listen to the sentences.

1 There are only two interesting buildings in the area around Newport.

2 The Green Belt should definitely be protected from developers.

5 Underline the stressed syllables in sentences from the listening excerpts in this unit. Use the audioscript at the back of your book. Then listen and check.

Check!

6 Do the crossword. All of the words are in Student's Book Unit 3.

Across

5 poor

8 past, present, or future

9 opposite of 5 across

10 small and neat

11 attached to the bedroom

Down

1 new, current

2 slightly (2 words)

3 appear

4 with a lot of room

6 lively

7 discussion

Unit 4 Innovation

4a The Boring Company

Listening future transportation

1 ▶ 28 Why do you think someone would name their company "The Boring Company"? What does this have to do with future transportation? Listen to a radio feature and check your answers.

2 ▶ 28 Listen again and answer the questions. According to the speaker:

1 what are the three possibilities for overcoming an obstacle?

_____

2 what can building new roads be compared to, and why?

_____

3 what is the problem with building "roads in the air"?

_____

4 what is the problem with building roads underground?

_____

5 how would cars travel in Elon Musk's proposed underground system?

_____

6 how would he make the tunneling process cheaper?

_____

7 what technology might the Hyperloop tunnel use in the future?

_____

8 how fast can pods travel in this system?

_____

3 ▶ 28 Complete these sentences and phrases used by the speaker. You have been given the first letter and a definition of the missing words. Listen again and check your answers.

1 We've already tried going around it by building **b**_____ **roads** around our cities …

= roads that take you around the edge of a city

2 … have an impact on those below when **d**_____ falls from a height.

= pieces of broken material, e.g., rock

3 And given his amazing record … he could **p**_____ this **off**.

= make something a success

4 His latest **v**_____ , The Boring Company, proposes building a network of tunnels …

= a business enterprise or project involving risk

5 … so that there would be nothing to block them or **h**_____ them **up**.

= delay

6 … Hyperloop project, has already been **t**_____ **and tested** …

= experimented with and shown to work

vacuum (n) /ˈvækjuəm/ a space that has had all the air removed from it
sled (n) /sled/ a small vehicle that slides over the ground

Grammar future probability

4 ▶ 28 Complete the statements made by the speaker with these words. Then listen again and check your answers.

could   good chance   likely   might   possibly   should

1 … such solutions are never _____ to work because …

2 … rather than removing the problem, you _____ just be moving it somewhere else.

3 … collisions or accidents in the air _____ also have an impact on those below …

4 And given his amazing record …, there's a _____ that he could pull this off.

5 Musk's idea is that … his techniques _____ reduce the cost enormously.

6 In his mind, also, is the idea that in the future, the tunnels will _____ use vacuum technology …

5 Rewrite the sentences from Exercise 4 so that they have the same meaning. Use the words in bold.

probably

1 _____

chances

2 _____

possible

3 _____

may well

4 _____

likely

5 _____

could

6 _____

6 Complete the answers to these questions about future transportation using the correct form of the words in parentheses.

Do you think that there's any chance this idea of Elon Musk's will become a reality?

It ¹_____ (could). I think he ²_____ (almost certainly / come up with) a working model. Then it will be a question of whether city authorities are willing to support it. I think that some more forward-looking ones ³_____ (probably / be) supportive of it.

And, just leaving aside that possibility, what do you think our city streets will look like thirty years from now?

I think most of us ⁴_____ (likely / drive) electric vehicles. We're already moving in that direction. So we ⁵_____ (should / have) cleaner air in our cities. But there ⁶_____ (probably / be) some gas cars on the streets, too.

Why do you say that?

Because the oil companies are incredibly powerful. And that ⁷_____ (be / unlikely / change).

Wordbuilding *-able*

7 Form the correct (positive or negative) adjective from the verb in parentheses to complete these sentences. The negative adjectives can begin with *un-*, *in-*, *ir-*, or *non-*.

1 I think it's _____ (do). The question is: Is it _____ (desire)?

2 I'm afraid the price is _____ (negotiate).

3 They're an advertising agency and they have this terrible slogan: "Imagine the _____ (imagine)"!

4 I felt so bad about breaking her plate. She said it was rare and virtually _____ (replace).

5 There are problems with the plan, but I don't think they are _____ (surmount).

6 I can't go through another dental procedure. The pain was _____ (tolerate).

8 Complete these sentences with a suitable adjective ending in *-able*.

1 If you don't like the shirt, I'm sure you can take it back to the store. Things are usually _____ within two weeks of buying them.

2 These new glasses are supposed to be _____ , but I sat on them and they snapped in half!

3 The tap water is _____ in the sense that it's safe. But it tastes awful.

4 How far is the station from here? Is it _____ , or should I get a bus or taxi?

5 The label on this tablecloth says "_____ ," but I actually put it in the washing machine and it came out fine.

6 I'm afraid I won't be _____ for the next few days; my hotel has no Wi-Fi.

4b DIY innovators

Reading **future transportation**

1 Read the article about DIY innovators and match the headings (a–d) with the four paragraphs (1–4).

  a What drives innovation ____

  b An unidentified need ____

  c Making do with bits and pieces ____

  d There's an inventor in all of us ____

2 Read the article again and complete these sentences using one word in each blank.

  1 The mistake we make about technology is that we think it is something only _____ can be involved with.

  2 Thomas Jefferson's clock was unusual for its time because it could tell you the _____ .

  3 The invention of eyeglasses for chickens solved something most people didn't think was a _____ .

  4 Most DIY inventors are not really motivated by _____ .

  5 In the Great Depression, some people created homemade versions of gadgets that they couldn't _____ .

  6 Robert Goddard is an example of a scientist who did _____ using old household objects.

DIY (abbrev) /ˌdiː aɪ ˈwaɪ/ do it yourself
peck (v) /pek/ (of a bird) strike quickly with the mouth
hose (n) /həʊz/ a flexible water pipe
scaffold (n) /ˈskæfəʊld/ a supporting structure used when repairing a building
piston rings (n) /ˈpɪstən rɪŋz/ metal rings that go around the cylinder of an internal combustion engine

DIY innovators

1 In today's electronic convenience age, many of us imagine that technology is something that brainy scientists in state-of-the-art laboratories create for us. But that isn't really a true reflection of how technology comes about—now or in the past. The strict definition of technology is designing a device to perform a particular task. Seen like that, we are all innovators because we have all, at one time or another, improvised our own solutions to specific problems. It's just that some of us take it further than others. The United States' third president, Thomas Jefferson, filled his home with DIY gadgets. In his living room, for example, he had a homemade clock which, using a pair of cannonballs on ropes, told him both the hour of the day and the day of the week. He made himself a swiveling seat—an early version of the type of office chair many of us sit on today—and built an automatic signing machine so that he **didn't need to hand-sign** his letters.

2 DIY inventions rarely catch on because often the inventor is providing a solution to something that is not generally perceived to be a problem. What was the inventor of glasses for chickens thinking? Obviously he thought there needed to be some way to prevent chickens from pecking at each other's eyes. But he **should have realized** that they were never going to become a best-seller. Similarly, the self-tipping hat, which used parts of a clock to tip a man's hat when a lady passed him in the street, **must have seemed** to fill a need that was obvious to the inventor.

3 While a few DIY innovators in the past **might have been motivated** by money and the dream of making their fortune, others have been motivated by necessity. World War II servicemen in North Africa who **needed to wash** took empty oil drums and hoses, mounted them on scaffolds built from scrap wood, and created improvised showers. Others have been motivated by economic hardship. During the Great Depression of the 1930s, some people **had to build** their own devices and equipment, because they couldn't afford new items in the stores. Cecil Burrell, when he wanted tables for his patio, made them from old piston rings from industrial engines.

4 But DIY can extend to professional scientists, too. Dr. Robert Goddard, who pioneered modern rocketry in the 1920s and 1930s, built much of his test equipment and rockets from bits and pieces he found lying around: clock parts, tobacco tins, etc.

3 Look at the words in bold from the article. Circle the correct definition (a or b).

1 a **swiveling** seat
  a turning   b with arms

2 rarely **catch on**
  a work   b become popular

3 to **tip** a man's hat
  a take off   b raise

4 **mounted** them **on** scaffolds
  a hang … from   b put … on top of

5 **scrap** wood
  a old but reusable b old and useless

6 who **pioneered** modern rocketry
  a was ignorant of b led the way in

Grammar past modals

4 Match the past modal verbs (1–6) from the article with the functions (a–f).

1 didn't need to hand-sign _____

2 should have realized _____

3 must have seemed _____

4 might have been motivated _____

5 needed to wash _____

6 had to build _____

a expresses what was expected

b describes an obligation

c talks about a necessity

d talks about a lack of necessity

e speculates about what was possibly the case

f speculates about what was probably the case

5 Read the story in the next column about someone who got a bicycle puncture. Rewrite the underlined phrases with past modal verbs.

1 _____

2 _____

3 _____

4 _____

5 _____

6 _____

7 _____

So there I was on a country road in the middle of nowhere with a flat bicycle tire. [1] Almost certainly I had ridden over a nail or something. [2] The advisable thing would have been to take a puncture repair kit with me, but because the roads are very new around there, I had imagined [3] it wasn't necessary. [4] One possibility was to wheel my bike back to the nearest town six kilometers away, but that would have taken a long time. Besides, [5] I had an obligation to be home for dinner, as a friend was coming over. So I decided [6] it was my duty to find a way to fix the puncture. All I had with me was a bicycle pump. What I needed was a patch for the puncture. I looked around on the road. [7] Perhaps someone had dropped something I could use. After some searching, I found some old chewing gum stuck to the road. It was very hard, and I realized that there was only one thing to do …

6 Pronunciation weak forms in past modals

a ▶ 29 Listen to these sentences. Circle the weak forms.

1 I shouldn't have bothered.

2 She may have gotten lost.

3 You didn't need to wait for me.

4 It might not have been his fault.

5 She had to leave early.

b Practice saying the sentences in Exercise 6a in the same way.

Vocabulary phrasal verb come

7 Complete the text using prepositions to make phrasal verbs with *come*.

We've all eaten popcorn at the movies, but few stop to think how the success of this all-American snack came [1] _____ . I came [2] _____ an article about its origins the other day when browsing the internet. It has an interesting history. The Guatemalans discovered popcorn thousands of years ago, presumably when someone had the bright idea of putting a corn kernel in a hot pan. But popcorn didn't really take off in the United States until the invention of the popcorn machine in the 1890s. Manufacturers spotted the growing trend and came [3] _____ with the idea of adding caramel and marketing it as the sweet snack many of us have come [4] _____ know and love. In the Depression of the 1930s, popcorn filled an important need because it was cheap. Since then, even though popcorn has come [5] _____ against some opponents who say that it is unhealthy, it remains very popular and is even marketed today as a health food.

4c The new philanthropists

Listening supporting good causes

1 ▶30 You are going to listen to a conversation about philanthropists. Read the definition. Then listen and take notes.

> **philanthropist** (n) /fɪˈlænθrəpɪst/ a person who cares about their fellow human beings; especially one who donates money to people less fortunate than themselves

1 two ways these new philanthropists made their money

_____

_____

2 two ways their approach to giving differs from philanthropists in the past

_____

_____

2 ▶30 Listen again. Are the sentences true (T) or false (F)?

1	The speaker implies that philanthropists in the past didn't have to work for their money.	T F
2	The new philanthropists' attitude toward their money is that they want to use it now.	T F
3	The new philanthropists don't want the projects they invest in to be run by businesspeople.	T F
4	The Daniela Papi story shows how a social enterprise project can evolve and spread.	T F
5	John Caudwell believes that success in life is just a question of hard work.	T F
6	The speaker suggests that the new philanthropists ultimately care only about their business reputation.	T F

3 ▶30 Complete these phrases from the conversation. Then listen again and check your answers.

> bring about   counterparts   ethos   return
> seed money   self-made   no strings

1 … so many more of these do-gooders are _____ businessmen and women …

2 … these philanthropists and their 19th-century _____ …

3 … business terms like "getting a good _____ on capital" …

4 The money they put into philanthropic projects is like _____ …

5 … helping _____ positive change in areas where social problems exist.

6 … none of the old-fashioned "_____ attached" kind of giving …

7 I'd say that was very typical of the _____ of the new philanthropists.

4 Write the words from Exercise 3 next to the correct definition.

1 set of beliefs and values _____

2 early investment in a new company

_____

3 profit _____

4 make happen _____

5 succeeding without help _____

6 someone who does the same job in a different time or place _____

7 without special conditions _____

Word focus *give*

5 Complete the expressions with *give*.

1 I **gave it my** _____ , but I didn't win—he was a much better player.

2 It's not a decision you can take lightly. You need to **give it some serious** _____ .

3 **Give her a** _____ . She's only 12. I didn't know what I wanted to do until I was 20!

4 I've never tried to steer a boat before, but I'll **give it a** _____ .

5 Don't rush it. You broke your leg. You need to **give it some** _____ to heal properly.

4d An elevator pitch

Real life making a short pitch

1 ▶ 31 Listen to a short pitch for a product called the "Solidarity Bag." Listen and answer the questions.

1 Who is the product aimed at?

_____

2 What is unique about this idea?

_____

3 What problem does it solve?

_____

4 What features does the bag have?

_____

2 Speaking skill using rhetorical questions

▶ 31 Listen again and complete these rhetorical questions.

1 What's _____ _____ about that, you _____ ?

2 Why _____ children _____ to do _____ , when they have a desk at school and a table at home?

3 But _____ will _____ in poorer countries _____ _____ to afford the bag?

3 Write the answers to the questions in Exercise 2.

1 _____

2 _____

3 _____

_____

4 Complete these other rhetorical questions you might ask when pitching a new product or service.

1 Operation
So how _____ ?

2 Cost
Isn't _____ , you ask?

3 Need
So why _____ ?

4 Ambition/Goal
So, what _____ ?

5 Pronunciation word stress

▶ 32 Look at the words in bold in these sentences and underline where you think the stress falls in each word. Then listen and check.

1 **Clearly**, we want to help others.
2 **Financially**, we are in a good position.
3 **Essentially**, it's a school backpack.
4 **Of course**, this is not the finished design.
5 **Honestly**, I don't know the answer to that.
6 **Obviously**, not all kids need this bag.
7 **To be honest**, I think people will pay extra.
8 **Basically**, we'd like to help kids learn.

6 Listen and respond defending your idea

▶ 33 Imagine you have just presented this Solidarity Bag to a potential investor. Listen to their questions. Respond with your own words. Then compare what you say with the model answer that follows.

1

> Can you just explain to me what your ambition is for this product?

> Yes. We would like it to have successful sales in Europe and on the basis of that to be able to provide many of these bags to children in developing countries.

4e Problem or solution?

Writing a proposal

1 Read the proposal and answer the questions.

1 Does the company currently recognize the importance of innovation, and if so, how?

_____

2 What specific, concrete suggestions does the proposal make?

_____

_____

3 What recommendations does it make without giving specific examples?

_____

_____

2 Answer these questions about the structure of the proposal.

1 What is the purpose of the introduction?

_____

2 In what two ways does the author make a list of points?

_____

_____

3 What phrase does she use to signal the conclusion?

_____

3 Writing skill making recommendations

Circle the correct options to complete the recommendations.

1 We suggest employees *be / to be* given a structure in which to innovate.

2 We recommend that the company *could / should* reward employees for their ideas.

3 We strongly recommend *to give / giving* innovation a more formal position.

4 We recommend that employees *have / having* scheduled discussion opportunities.

5 We also suggest that they *are to visit / should visit* other organizations to get ideas.

Introduction
This proposal suggests a new way to encourage innovation and creativity among staff.

Current situation
Our company needs innovation to be successful. At the moment, although we say that "we encourage creativity and innovation," in fact we receive very few ideas from employees about how to improve our products and processes. Innovation is important because it can:

- help make the company more efficient
- create new products and services
- motivate staff
- help secure the company's future

So how can we achieve more creativity and innovation in practice, not just in words?

Possible solutions
First of all, we suggest that employees should be given a structure in which to innovate. This could take the form of a scheduled discussion between groups of colleagues every two to four weeks. Or it could involve giving employees the opportunity to visit other organizations to see how they work. Secondly, we recommend rewarding employees for good ideas. This does not have to be a financial reward, but it must involve recognition of their effort. Lastly, we believe that creating a more relaxed relationship between employees and management would also help the flow of ideas.

Recommendations
In summary, we strongly recommend that innovation and creativity be given a more formal position in the company's working practices.

4 Use these notes to write a proposal for a way to make students more aware of ways we waste energy.

Problem: Students are conscious of the dangers of pollution, but not of their own waste of energy (leaving on lights, phone chargers, etc.).

Possible solutions: awareness-raising campaign, fines for wasting energy, offer free "green" charging devices

Wordbuilding partitives

1 Complete the partitive expressions using these words. Use a dictionary if necessary.

bit	bite	drop	gust	hint
plot	shred	stroke	word	

1 I'm really thirsty. I haven't had **a _____ of water** all day.

2 It was **a _____ of luck** getting those tickets. They were the last two.

3 I'm sorry. I didn't mean to offend you. It was just **a _____ of fun**.

4 **A** sudden **_____ of wind** blew my hat off, and it landed in a puddle.

5 He tried to be positive, but I think there was **a _____ of disappointment** in his voice.

6 They bought **a _____ of land** near the sea, and they intend to build a house there.

7 Can I give you **a _____ of advice** before you start out on this venture?

8 There's not **a _____ of evidence** to suggest that there is life on other planets.

9 We'll get **a _____ to eat** when we get there.

2 Which four expressions in Exercise 1 emphasize a small amount?

a _____

b _____

c _____

d _____

Learning skills vocabulary extension (1)

3 You can use your dictionary to extend your vocabulary. If you see a word that you think you know but the meaning does not seem to fit, check the other meanings of this word in the dictionary. Look at this example.

1 You see this sentence but don't know this meaning of *capital*.

"Running a railway network is a very capital-intensive activity."

2 You find these entries for *capital* in the dictionary. Which meaning does it have in this sentence?

capital /ˈkæpɪt(ə)l/ noun
1 the administrative center of a country or region
2 money or assets that are or can be invested

capital /ˈkæpɪt(ə)l/ adjective
3 (of a letter of the alphabet) large
4 (of punishment or crime) punishable by death

3 Note any new meanings in your notebook and write an example sentence for each one.

4 Look at these words with more than one meaning. What meanings do you know for each?

crane	fair	fine	sole

5 Read the sentences. Do you know the meanings of the words in bold in these sentences? Check other meanings in the dictionary. Write example sentences for the meanings that are new to you.

1 In Japan, a popular origami shape is a paper **crane**.

2 I went to the Frankfurt book **fair** last week.

3 There's a **fine** line between confidence and arrogance.

4 It's not a company: he is a **sole** trader.

Check!

6 Answer these questions. All the answers are in Student Book Unit 4.

1 What is the "mother of invention"? _____

2 What adjective describes gadgets you can fold? "_____ technology"

3 What type of eye did you see on the opening page of this unit? _____

4 What is the name for a short presentation where we have a limited time to convince someone of our idea? _____

5 What do we call someone who wants to make money but also helps people? _____

7 Complete the sentences. The first letter of each word spell the name of Blake Mycoskie's company.

1 I'll certainly give your idea some _____ .

2 It's _____ a very risky venture. I'll be surprised if it comes through.

3 Tina won the "Entrepreneur of the Year" award. She _____ be thrilled.

4 To make something smaller, you can _____ it, bend it, or fold it.

Name of company: _____

Unit 5 The magic of travel

5a In defense of the guided tour

Listening a traveler's view

1 ▶ 34 Look at these features of organized tours. Think about which features appeal to you and which don't. Then listen to someone talking about the benefits of such tours and check (✓) the items he mentions.

1 Being with knowledgeable guides ☐
2 Comfort and safety ☐
3 Meeting fellow travelers ☐
4 Having a fixed itinerary/schedule ☐
5 No planning—everything is arranged ☐
6 Known costs—no financial surprises ☐
7 Optional free time ☐

2 ▶ 34 Read the statements. Then listen again and circle the best answer (a, b, or c) to complete each statement.

1 The speaker says that he joined the guided tour at the Metropolitan Museum of Art because:
   a he thought it would at least be a new experience.
   b it was still raining outside.
   c it was highly recommended by the museum staff.

2 The difference between the museum tour and one of his normal visits to a museum was that:
   a he learned a lot about a lot of things.
   b he learned a little about a lot of things.
   c he learned a lot about a few things.

3 Most of the guides on the Italy trip:
   a had also been guests on the trips before.
   b had done months of research before the trip.
   c had academic qualifications.

4 The speaker says the fact that everything is organized beforehand saves a lot of:
   a money.   b stress.   c time.

5 The speaker says many organized tour operators these days give their guests:
   a the option of more free time.
   b a choice of excursions to go on.
   c mini guided tours with local people.

3 Try to complete these expressions used by the speaker. Use one word per blank.

1 to be herded around like a _____
2 Never in a _____ years!
3 Don't get me _____—I like museums.
4 It'll be an experience, if _____ else.
5 Not holding _____ much hope, I joined it.
6 Transportation, hotels, food: it's all taken care _____ .

Vocabulary repeated word pairs

4 Complete these repeated word pairs with the correct word.

1 She only had her operation a week ago, but she's getting better day _____ day.
2 The movie went on _____ on. I thought it was never going to end.
3 Yes, we met face _____ face for the first time last week.
4 People ask if I prefer writing the music or lyrics, but actually they go hand _____ hand.
5 Their new business is going _____ strength _____ strength.
6 We don't see eye _____ eye on a lot of issues, but we're still good friends.

Grammar emphatic structures

5 ▶ 34 Use the words in parentheses to rewrite the sentences with emphatic structures you heard in Exercise 1. Then listen again and check your answers.

1 I want a little independence from travel. (what)

_____

2 A guided tour I took changed my mind. (thing)

_____

3 I like visiting museums. (do)

_____

4 It made me reassess my whole attitude toward organized tours. (did)

_____

5 How knowledgeable and interesting some of the other travelers were surprised me. (what)

_____

6 ... particularly if you're visiting a more remote or not-so-safe place. (it)

_____

6 Read this account of family vacations. Rewrite the underlined sentences below as emphatic structures, using the words in parentheses.

[1] I remember best about my childhood how amazing family vacations were. Every few years, we took a camper van and set off somewhere new. We didn't have a strict itinerary. [2] A rough idea of where we were going was enough. We just took things day by day, without any planned stops or schedule. [3] We stopped when we saw things that interested us. We went wild swimming. We usually cooked on our camp stove. [4] Money wasn't an issue. If we saw a restaurant that looked good, we'd stop and eat there. [5] I loved the lack of any kind of routine. Sometimes we'd wake up early, sometimes late. We'd often take a nap in the afternoon at some scenic spot. The whole thing was magical. [6] When I have children, I'm going to re-create a similar experience for them.

1 _____ (thing)
2 _____ (it)
3 _____ (did)
4 _____ (it)
5 _____ (what)
6 _____ (what)

7 Pronunciation *do, does,* and *did*

▶ 35 Listen to these sentences and write the missing emphatic auxiliaries. Note how the auxiliary verbs are stressed.

1 I _____ wish I had been able to spend more time there.

2 He _____ say that he'd help us.

3 We _____ prefer to take vacations close to home.

4 She _____ get very sunburned.

Vocabulary describing people and places

8 Do the crossword using the clues below.

Across
1 warm and comfortable
4 not fast
7 evoking feelings of love

Down
2 using authority in a self-important way
3 stylish and graceful
5 cautious or suspicious
6 large and impressive

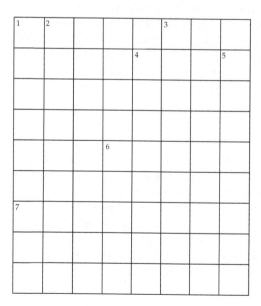

5b Pilgrimages

Reading their Africa

1 Read the article about the Pilgrimages project and answer the questions.

1 What is the aim of the Pilgrimages project?

_____

2 What inspired the project?

_____

3 How are the books different from the usual travel books we read?

_____

_____

4 What are the writers trying to avoid?

_____

2 Read the article again and find words with these meanings.

a randomly (para 1) _____

b take hold of firmly (para 1) _____

c easily noticed (para 2) _____

d troubled (para 3) _____

e a picture (para 3) _____

f unoriginal (para 4) _____

g announce an order (para 4) _____

Pilgrimages

"For one month, nearly a billion eyes will follow the wayward movement of one small ball, bouncing about haphazardly on a lawn—controlled by the feet of 22 men speaking a language billions understand very well." These are the opening words on the Pilgrimages website, a project set up by the Chinua Achebe Centre for African Writers and Artists, to seize the opportunity presented by the soccer World Cup in South Africa in 2010 to educate the rest of the world about Africa. The way the **association** did this was to ask thirteen African writers to write about their experiences of thirteen cities spread across Africa. Each **author** had two years, and help from a local guide, to produce a book of approximately 30,000 words on each city.

The result is travel writing of a very different kind. Rather than experiencing a place through the eyes of an outsider, Pilgrimages aims to reveal **it** as seen by Africans themselves. The advantage for each writer is that although they are visiting cities previously not well known to them, many things are already familiar to them. **This** means that they can concentrate on observing the details and while **doing so**, not be as conspicuous as a non-African visitor **would**. Ugandan author Doreen Baingana, whose subject is the Somalian city of Hargeisa, says: "Goats in a city, for example, do not surprise me in the way they would if I were from the U.K."

Among the **other thirteen** is Yvonne Owuor of Kenya, who has written about Kinshasa, the capital of the Democratic Republic of Congo. The city is a great mix of different African cultures and languages with a turbulent history of colonization and struggle for independence. Like other Pilgrimages writers, Owuor is cautious about painting her portrait of Kinshasa with too broad a brush, fearful that what will emerge is a one-dimensional, stereotyped view of Africa.

This promises to be a refreshing series of travel books: not **ones** that throw out clichéd images and stereotyped views of other worlds. As Owuor says, when writers decree that a given place is like this or like that, then the reality disappears from view.

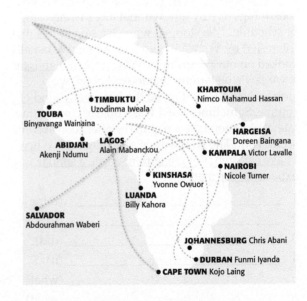

TOUBA
Binyavanga Wainaina

● TIMBUKTU
Uzodinma Iweala

ABIDJAN
Akenji Ndumu

LAGOS
Alain Mabanckou

SALVADOR
Abdourahman Waberi

● KINSHASA
Yvonne Owuor

LUANDA
Billy Kahora

KHARTOUM
Nimco Mahamud Hassan

HARGEISA
Doreen Baingana

● KAMPALA Victor Lavalle

● NAIROBI
Nicole Turner

JOHANNESBURG Chris Abani

● DURBAN Funmi Iyanda

● CAPE TOWN Kojo Laing

Grammar avoiding repetition

3 Look at the words in bold in the article and answer the questions.

   1 What words have these words replaced to avoid repetition?

     a association (para 1) _____

     b author (para 1) _____

   2 What clauses do these words refer to?

     a This (para 2) _____

     b doing so (para 2) _____

   3 What nouns do these words refer to?

     a it (para 2, line 3) _____

     b This (para 4, line 1) _____

     c ones (para 4) _____

   4 What words have been omitted after these words?

     a would (para 2) _____

     b other thirteen (para 3) _____

4 Replace the underlined words with other words or omit the underlined words to avoid repetition.

   1 I was going to buy a new umbrella, but then I found my old <u>umbrella</u>.

     _____

   2 I didn't want to go, but he persuaded me <u>to go</u>.

     _____

   3 I want to call her to find out what's going on, but if I <u>call her</u>, she might think I'm being pushy.

     _____

   4 I downloaded all the Bob Marley songs, but I didn't bother with the <u>other songs</u>.

     _____

   5 The temperature is expected to drop to zero degrees tonight. <u>The temperature dropping to zero degrees</u> means there will be a frost.

     _____

   6 It's a brilliant company. You couldn't find a better <u>company</u> to work for.

     _____

   7 I'd love you to give me a hand moving this table, if you can bear <u>to give me a hand</u>.

     _____

   8 It's not a cheap solution, but I understand why you might think <u>it is a cheap solution</u>.

     _____

5 Pronunciation stress in short responses

a ▶ 36 Look at these exchanges. Mark the two (or three) words that you think are most stressed in each response (B). Then listen and check.

   1 A: Would you like to come to dinner some evening?

     B: Yes, I'd love to.

   2 A: Do you need to borrow a pen?

     B: No, I have one, thanks.

   3 A: Are you coming?

     B: No, I'm afraid not.

   4 A: I didn't get the assistant manager job.

     B: Oh, I'm sorry to hear that.

   5 A: Are you going away this summer?

     B: I hope so.

   6 A: Do you like detective stories?

     B: Oh, yes. I love a good thriller.

   7 A: What are you doing here so early?

     B: Catching up on emails.

b ▶ 37 Listen to Speaker A's part of the exchanges. Respond using the correct stress.

6 Dictation a mystery tour

▶ 38 Listen to someone describing a mystery tour. Complete the paragraph.

I've been _____,

but _____ in Prague

_____.

And _____

_____.

If you _____,

_____.

I'm _____

_____

because _____

_____.

What _____

_____.

If _____

_____!

5c Heart of Darkness

Listening a voyage into the unknown

1 ▶ 39 You are going to listen to an excerpt from the book *Heart of Darkness* by Joseph Conrad. The setting is the Congo around 1880. The excerpt describes the beginning of the journey that Marlow, a ship's captain, makes to this area. Listen and answer the questions.

1 What did Marlow dream about as a boy?

_____

2 What had happened to the place he had been most fascinated by?

_____

3 How did his dream become a reality?

_____

2 ▶ 39 Listen again and complete these details of the description.

1 What was found on maps of the world at that time?

_____

2 In contrast, what had the map of this place (Congo) become filled with?

_____

3 What does he compare the river on the map to?

_____

4 What had happened to the captain that Marlow was replacing?

_____

5 What was his impression of the African coast?

_____

3 Look at these sentences from the excerpts and answer the questions about the descriptive words in bold.

1 I would look for hours at South America, or Africa, or Australia, and **lose myself in** all the glories of exploration.

Do you think *lose myself in something* has a positive or a negative connotation?

_____

2 But there was one [place] yet—the biggest, the most blank—that **I had a hankering after**.

Have people who hanker after something experienced it yet or not?

_____

3 I went on along Fleet Street, but could not **shake off** the idea.

Which of these things would you not try to shake off?

a a cold   b a new skill   c a bad reputation

4 Watching a coast as it slips by the ship is like thinking about **an enigma**.

Do you think *an enigma* is:

a a mystery?   b a new idea?

5 … and always **mute** with an air of whispering …

If *blind* means "cannot see" and *deaf* means "cannot hear," what does *mute* mean?

_____

Word focus *matter*

4 Circle the correct options to complete these phrases with *matter*.

1 Getting stuck in an elevator underground might seem amusing, but believe me, at the time, **it was no** *joking / funny / laughing* **matter.**

2 They say that you can control pain; it's just a question of *brain / mind / will* **over matter.**

3 You should always use a safety belt, **as a matter of** *course / process / mode.*

4 I'm sorry—I'm vegetarian. I don't eat meat **as a matter of** *belief / principle / morals.*

5 **No matter which** *angle / point / way* **you look at it**, being a teenager isn't easy.

6 Thankfully, it's not my concern; or yours **for** *that / any / what* **matter.**

5d To my amazement

Real life telling an anecdote

1 ▶ 40 Listen to an anecdote about hitchhiking and answer the questions.

1 Where were the two men hitchhiking to, and why?

_____

2 What piece of good luck did they have?

_____

3 What happened to change their mood for the worse, and how did the story end?

_____

2 ▶ 40 Listen again and complete these phrases that link or introduce the events in the story.

1 Very few people still hitchhike
_____ .

2 _____ it can be dangerous.

3 _____ , a group of us from our university had a competition …

4 _____ , within about ten minutes … we got a ride …

5 We couldn't _____ our luck.

6 … a rest stop, which _____ , _____ to have an area for pitching tents.

7 _____ , we woke up early …

8 … but, to _____ , it had left.

9 _____ , we started to pack up our tent.

10 But _____ , we heard a loud horn.

3 Speaking skill linking events

Substitute these phrases for a similar phrase from Exercise 2.

a As luck would have it, … ——

b Just then, … ——

c Despondently, … ——

d Nowadays, … ——

e To our great surprise, … ——

f Last summer, … ——

g The next day, … ——

h To our horror, … ——

4 Pronunciation long vowel sounds

a Look at the underlined vowel sounds in these words and put them in the correct place in the chart below.

amazement   consequence   astonishment
delight   dismay   embarrassment
frustration   horror   regret
relief   shock   surprise

Long vowel sound	Short vowel sound

b ▶ 41 Listen and check your answers. Say each word after you hear it.

5 Listen and respond telling an anecdote

▶ 42 You are going to tell a story about falling asleep on a train and ending up in the wrong place. A friend will ask you some questions. Respond with your own words. Then compare what you say with the model answer that follows.

1

So, tell me what happened.

Well, a couple of weeks ago, I took the train to go and visit my aunt in Newville.

5e Book of the month

Writing a review

1 Read this book review of *The Siege of Krishnapur* by J.G. Farrell and mark the parts of the review that do the following:

1 describe the setting and the plot
2 describe the theme of the book
3 describe the style of writing
4 give the reader's opinion of the book

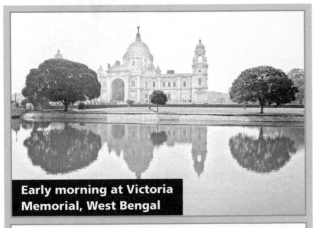

Early morning at Victoria Memorial, West Bengal

It is 1857, and the British Empire in India is facing severe unrest from the indigenous population. For the ruling British class in the northern town of Krishnapur, life is calm and polite until the sepoys at a nearby military fort rise in mutiny and the British are forced to retreat into the British Residency. Food and other supplies become short, disease sets in, and the inhabitants' resources are tested to the limit.

This is the first part of J.G. Farrell's empire trilogy, an examination of the British Empire in its decline. *The Siege of Krishnapur* serves as a metaphor for this decline as each character is forced to examine their own view of the world.

Although the situation is desperate, Farrell describes it with great elegance and humor, conveying the ridiculousness of the British position. Some would argue that in not describing the hardship and injustice suffered by the local Indian population, Farrell has done them a great injustice. But I do not think that was his aim. What he has done is to write both a gripping story and a thought-provoking study of colonial life.

2 Which of these techniques (a–e) has the writer used to begin this review?

a giving an opinion about the book directly
b talking about the writer's background
c describing the opening of the story
d giving a short summary of the whole story
e discussing the topic or theme of the book

3 Writing skill **descriptive words**

Complete the definitions of words describing books and writing with these words.

convincing	fetched	packed
poorly	provoking	uninspiring
uninspiring	wrenching	

1 A book that makes you think is a thought-_____ book.
2 A story in which a lot of exciting events happen is action-_____ .
3 A story in which nothing much happens is _____ .
4 A plot that is very difficult to believe is far-_____ .
5 A fictional character who you believe could really exist is _____ .
6 An ending that is extremely sad is heart-_____ .
7 A book that is kind of dull and flat is _____ .
8 The opposite of *well-written* is _____ written.

4 Think of a novel you have read and write two short alternative opening paragraphs. For the first, give a short summary of the whole story. For the second, discuss the topic or theme of the book.

1 _____
_____
_____
_____
_____

2 _____
_____
_____
_____
_____

Wordbuilding synonyms

1 Complete these sentences using a synonym for the underlined word. You have been given the first two letters of the missing words.

1 It's a very picturesque <u>place</u> and a great sp_____ for a picnic.

2 I didn't <u>succeed in</u> finding cooking chocolate, but I ma_____ to get some ordinary chocolate.

3 It didn't <u>spoil</u> my enjoyment of the book generally, but it ru_____ the ending.

4 I was told Rome would be <u>wonderful</u>, and it was. The city was truly ma_____ .

5 Our <u>journey</u> into the Amazon got off to a bad start, but it was a tr_____ I'll never forget.

6 I had read that Celia was one of the more <u>popular</u> guides. After our tour, I could see why she was so we_____ .

7 We had <u>hopes</u> that the movie would do well, but it has surpassed all our ex_____ .

8 Can you <u>recognize</u> that figure on the left of the picture? I can't ma_____ it ou_____ .

9 We <u>started out</u> at 9 a.m., and the others se_____ of_____ an hour later.

10 The climb was <u>exhilarating</u>, and reaching the top was even more th_____ .

Learning skills vocabulary extension (2)

2 You can use pictures to extend your vocabulary. Follow these steps.

1 Find a picture that interests you and look at the objects in it. The picture could also include people's expressions, feelings, or actions that are happening.

2 See how many items you can name in English and then write the other words in your own language.

3 Look up the English equivalents of these words in a bilingual dictionary. Check the example sentences to see that the meaning is the same and check the pronunciation.

4 Now label five new items in the picture with words you have just learned.

5 Look at the picture thirty minutes later and test yourself. Can you remember the new words?

3 Look at the photo at the top of the page and follow the steps in Exercise 2. You will find a larger version of the photo on page 66 of your Student Book.

Check!

4 Complete these sentences about characters and events with the correct form of the words given. All the answers are in Student's Book Unit 5.

1 The travel writer in the Opener referred to a bad experience with an _____ museum curator in Paris. (official)

2 In 5a, the writer says his trip to Chile, where he stayed at a _____ lodge on a nature reserve, fulfilled his _____ . (sustain, expect)

3 In 5b, the speaker describes going on a _____ mystery tour to an _____ destination. (magic, know)

4 In 5c, the writer describes Hergé's *Tintin* books as _____ novels. (graph)

5 In 5c, we learn that Hergé was not just a great _____ but also a great storyteller. (cartoon)

6 In 5d, we looked at adverbial linking phrases like "to my _____" and "_____ ." (relieve, worry)

7 In 5e, the writer describes the *Bridge of San Luis Rey* as a _____-_____ book. (think, provoke)

8 In 5f, the writer describes a _____ experience that he had while walking in Spain. (transform)

Unit 6 Body matters

6a Here comes the sun

Listening a healing regime

1 ▶ 43 Listen to a man describing his search for an exercise regime to help him recover from an injury. Answer the questions.

1 Where did he travel to?

_____

2 What was he hoping to heal?

_____

3 Was the exercise regime successful?

_____

2 ▶ 43 Listen again. What is significant about each of these numbers in the story?

1 1968: the date when _____

2 hundreds of thousands: the number of _____
_____

3 200: the number of _____

4 6:50: the time when _____

5 two weeks: the length of _____

6 30 minutes: the length of time that _____
_____

3 Circle the correct synonym (a or b) for the words in bold from the excerpt.

1 … at least **put off** the day when I would have to face back surgery.

a postpone   b cancel

2 … it supports around 200 disadvantaged boys—some **orphaned** …

a without homes   b without parents

3 There were no other distractions—no New Age tunes playing, no yoga **outfits** …

a equipment   b special clothing

4 The yoga carried on in a **serene** way for two weeks, never causing me even to break a sweat.

a calm   b intense

5 The **persistent** pain hasn't entirely gone away, but it has subsided.

a constant   b irritating

6 I can now **put up with** it because I've given up worrying about it.

a tolerate   b forget

Grammar phrasal verbs

4 ▶ 43 Look at these phrasal verbs that the speaker uses. Then listen again and write the object of the transitive verbs. If there is no object, write *intransitive*.

1 turn up _____

2 end up _____

3 get over _____

4 put off _____

5 look for _____

6 pull in _____

7 put up _____

8 work on _____

9 carry on _____

10 put up with _____

11 give up _____

5 Answer these questions about the transitive phrasal verbs in Exercise 4.

1 Which verb is clearly a separable verb? _____

2 Which verb is clearly inseparable? _____

3 Of the rest, which do you think are separable and which inseparable?

_____

6 Add the pronouns to these sentences.

1 The pain is pretty bad, but I've learned to put up with. (it)

2 I got the injury playing soccer, and it took me a long time to get over. (it)

3 If you think going to yoga classes will help, then there's no point putting off. (it)

4 I used to ski a lot, but I gave up. (it)

5 Reducing the cost of the course for students really pulled in. (them)

6 Can you put up for the night on Tuesday when I'm in town? (me)

7 I'm not as limber as I used to be, but I put down to my age. (that)

8 I can't touch my toes yet, but I'm working on. (it)

Vocabulary **phrasal verbs**

7 Circle the correct phrasal verb to complete the definitions.

1 To *come across / come out of* something means "to find it unexpectedly."

2 To *set apart / set aside* money or time means "to reserve it."

3 To *pick up / take up* a new hobby or sport means "to begin practicing it."

4 To *put someone off / turn someone off* something means "to discourage them from doing it."

5 If something *takes off / lifts off*, it becomes successful.

6 To *get away from / get out of* a difficult task means "to avoid having to do it."

7 To *carry out / carry off* a task means "to perform it."

8 To *fall back on / go back on* something means "to use it as a reserve or backup."

Vocabulary **exercise and health**

8 Complete this conversation using one word in each space.

A: How do you ^{1} _____ so fit, Bella? Do you ^{2} _____ lots of exercise or something?

B: Not so much these days. I used to work ^{3} _____ at the gym twice a week, doing weights and running on the treadmill.

A: So what's the secret? How do you keep in such good ^{4} _____ ?

B: I think I'm just lucky, really. I've never been ^{5} _____ any kind of diet and I find that if I ^{6} _____ reasonably active, I don't really have to ^{7} _____ my weight.

A: I think that's my problem. I just never seem to find time to exercise.

9 Dictation **fitness crazes**

▶ 44 Listen to this conversation between two people about fitness classes. Complete the conversation.

A: The other day, _____
_____ .

B: Did you _____ ?

A: Not really. I didn't _____
_____ .

B: You mean like Zumba?

A: Yes. I knew Zumba _____ ,
_____ .

B: And do you? _____ ,

A: Yes, I do. _____
_____ .

6b Cross-training

Reading advice for athletes

1 Read the article and underline the three sentences that tell you the following:

1 the definition of cross-training
2 cross-training's most significant benefit
3 what cross-training teaches us

2 Read the article again and circle the correct option (a, b, or c).

1 The main benefit of swimming to a cyclist is to help them:

a relax.   b build muscle.   c have more stamina.

2 Marathon running is given as an example of a sport that is:

a anti-social.   b boring.   c lonely.

3 Cross-training helps athletes avoid injuries by adding:

a variety.   b gentler exercise.
c breaks from exercise.

4 The writer implies that an athlete's career is relatively:

a dangerous.   b short.   c easy.

5 The word *diet* in paragraph 3 could be replaced by:

a routine.   b menu.   c day.

6 The result of taking up a new form of exercise is that your body:

a becomes stressed.   b feels happy.
c gets stronger.

Cross-training

In recent years, there has been an increased focus among practitioners of all types of sports on cross-training. It has become in fact a critical part of most top athletes' regular routines. Simply put, cross-training **means practicing** other sports or forms of exercise to improve, indirectly, your abilities in your main or target sport. An example of this would be a cyclist going swimming a couple of times a week. Swimming **requires you to control** your breathing, and so it can also **help more generally to increase** a cyclist's endurance. It also **lets you build** strength in a more relaxed way because the support of the water puts less strain on joints and muscles.

There are several benefits to cross-training. First, it **tends to be** more interesting for the athlete to be engaged in different activities. If their sport is a solitary one, like marathon running, playing a team sport like soccer could provide a social aspect to their training. Second, it can strengthen and improve joints and muscles that are vital if they are to **succeed in performing** their sport at the highest level. Finally, and most importantly, it **prevents athletes from getting** the kind of repetitive strain injuries that they often suffer from if they only practice the same activities day in, day out. It can not only improve performance, but also extend an athlete's life. In recent years, several soccer players have used yoga to **enable them to continue playing** into their late thirties and even in some cases, their early forties.

Cross-training is not just useful for the elite sportsperson, either. It has benefits for all of us. To stay injury-free,

I **recommend everyone incorporate** the following elements into their exercise diet:

- two parts cardiovascular exercise (e.g., running, swimming, cycling, skipping, tennis)
- one part strength building (e.g., weight training)
- one part stretching (e.g., yoga, dance, aerobics)
- one part balance training (e.g., yoga, surfing, gymnastics)

The lesson of cross-training is that the body reacts well to new experiences. Each time you embark on a new form of exercise, whether it be weight-lifting or cycling, the body must **learn to deal with** new stresses and new demands. And in doing that, it will naturally strengthen.

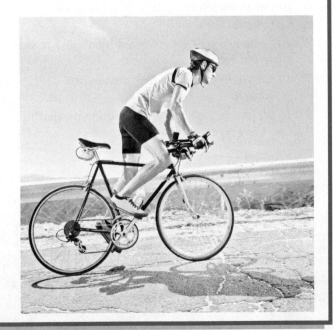

Grammar verb patterns

3 Look at these verb patterns (1–6). Complete the chart with examples of the verb patterns in bold from the article.

1 Verb + infinitive	_____
	_____
	_____
2 Verb + object + infinitive	_____
	_____
3 Verb + object + base form	_____
	_____
4 Verb + -ing	_____
5 Verb + preposition + -ing	_____
6 Verb + object + preposition + -ing	_____

4 Complete the sentences using the correct form of the verbs. You sometimes also need to use a preposition.

1 Many people forget _____ properly before exercising. (warm up)

2 Sports therapists encourage athletes _____ cross-training as a way to extend their careers. (do)

3 I don't recommend _____ more than one hour of intensive exercise a day. (do)

4 You can't make people _____ , but you can help them _____ the benefits. (exercise, see)

5 I miss _____ soccer, but at my age it's just not worth the risk of injury. (play)

6 If I worried _____ injured all the time, I would never try anything new. (get)

7 I thank my teacher _____ me interested in rowing. (get)

8 The best exercise routines seem _____ the ones that incorporate different elements of exercise. (be)

9 I started _____ tennis when I was ten, but then I switched to basketball. (play)

10 I love _____ sports, but I dislike _____ . (play, train)

Vocabulary injuries

5 Complete the sentences with the correct form of these verbs to make collocations.

| bruise | bump | chip | graze |
| lose | pull | sprain | stub |

1 He fell down in the playground and _____ **his knee**.

2 I got up during the night and _____ **my toe** on the bed leg.

3 I didn't notice how low the doorway was and I _____ **my head**.

4 I bit on the shell of a nut in my cereal and _____ **my tooth**.

5 The doctor said nothing was broken—I just _____ **my ribs**, apparently.

6 Sorry, I've _____ **my voice**. I was talking all day yesterday to a group of schoolchildren.

7 I stepped in a hole on the sidewalk and _____ **my ankle**.

8 I can't play tennis this weekend. I _____ **a muscle** in my shoulder the last time I played.

6 Complete these idioms with prepositions. Then replace the underlined expressions in the sentences with the idioms.

to be shaken _____   to be _____ the mend

to pass _____   to be run-_____

1 It was so hot in the room, I practically <u>fainted</u>. _____

2 I'm glad Pete's <u>getting better</u> now; he seems to have been sick for a long time. _____

3 I've been working solidly for months, and I'm very <u>lacking in energy</u>. _____

4 She felt very <u>distressed</u> by the incident, even though no one got hurt. _____

7 Pronunciation stress in two-syllable verbs

a ▶ 45 Circle the verbs that have stress on the second syllable. Which two do not? Then listen and check your answers.

admire	avoid	convince	delay	expect
insist	involve	postpone	practice	prevent
rely	require	succeed	welcome	

b What is the difference between the two verbs that have stress on the first syllable and the others?

6c The beauty industry

Listening globalizing beauty

1 ▶ 46 Listen to an interview with an expert on the fashion and beauty industry. Which of these statements (a, b, or c) best summarizes her views?

  a Globalization has made us all aspire to the same ideal of beauty.

  b Companies have come to realize that local traditions are important.

  c Companies try to convince us to want the same things because it's cheaper for them.

2 ▶ 46 Listen again and complete the examples that the speaker gives to illustrate the following points. Pause each time before moving onto the next question.

  1 General economic growth has affected our view of beauty.

    a The global cosmetics industry _____ _____ .

    b Americans _____ _____ .

  2 New markets keep being found.

    _____ brings in over $30 billion.

  3 In the early 20th century, cosmetics companies were peddling a Western and "white" ideal of beauty.

    Some promised that _____ _____ .

  4 The more recent era of globalization is one in which companies definitely have to be more conscious of local traditions and values.

    A company like _____ _____ .

  5 Multinational companies adapt their products to include local and traditional ingredients.

    a _____ for skin cleansing

    b the Huito fruit _____

3 Replace the words in bold from the interview with one-word synonyms.

  1 Has a globalized world made our ideal of beauty more **homogenized**?

  2 If you go back to the early 20th century … cosmetics companies were **peddling** a Western ideal of beauty.

  3 … if people everywhere could aspire to the same **notion** of beauty …

  4 … McDonald's **alters** its menu to suit the tastes of each local market …

  5 … a clear skin, healthy-looking hair, a youthful **glow** …

Word focus *face*

4 Complete this conversation using one word in each space.

A: Why the [1] _____ face? Are you upset about something?

B: Yes, I'm going to a school reunion and all my clothes make me look too old. The last time I saw all those people, I was 18!

A: Well, be careful. If you wear something that makes you look like you're obviously trying to look younger, no one will be able to **keep a** [2] _____ **face. Let's face** [3] _____ , none of them are going to be looking any younger, either.

B: I wouldn't bet on it. Sue Williamson always used to spend tons on her appearance. She looked fantastic the last time I saw her.

A: Well, I don't see what the big deal is. If she thinks she's going to [4] _____ **face** by looking old, that's her problem, not yours …

B: No, you're right. It's all very superficial. I'll just choose something nice and go and **face the** [5] _____ . If they want to make judgments, let them.

6d It'll do them good

Real life discussing proposals

1 ▶ 47 Listen to four speakers each discussing a different proposal for the workplace. Write the number of the speaker (1–4) next to the proposal they discuss (a–f). Note that there are two extra proposals.

_____ a   a way to help people feel less stressed

_____ b   a way to help people get more exercise

_____ c   a way to reduce car use

_____ d   a way to have a healthier atmosphere

_____ e   a way to help people eat more healthily

_____ f   a way to build team spirit

2 What was the specific proposal in each case?

1   do without a(n) _____

2   do without _____

3   provide (a) _____

4   provide opportunities for _____
_____

3 ▶ 47 Listen again and note down the possible problem with each proposal.

1   _____

2   _____

3   _____

4   _____

4 Speaking skill proposing and conceding a point

▶ 47 Complete the phrases the speakers used to propose and concede points. Then listen again and check your answers.

1   A better _____ would _____ to have just one, which can be a service elevator.

2   I _____ that sometimes people who have heavy things to move … will sometimes want to use the elevator, but we can _____ work _____ that.

3   It _____ be _____ better just to have straightforward fresh air sucked in from outside.

4   _____ , it wouldn't always be cool air, _____ it would be a lot healthier.

5   I haven't really thought _____ who should be responsible for making the list, but I do think …

6   I _____ not _____ will want to join in in that way, but for a lot of people, the social …

5 Pronunciation toning down negative statements

a ▶ 48 Listen and underline the words that have the most stress in these sentences.

1   I'm not very much in favor of the proposal.

2   It's not exactly what I had in mind.

3   It's not a particularly cheap option.

4   It hasn't proved to be so successful.

5   I'm not entirely convinced.

b Practice saying each sentence in Exercise 5a in the same way.

6 Listen and respond giving your opinion

▶ 49 Imagine you are at a meeting to discuss a proposal to install a gym in your workplace to help staff keep fit. Your colleagues ask you questions. Respond with your own words. Then compare what you say with the model answer that follows.

1
> What do you think of the proposal?

> I think it's a great idea. It would really help staff to keep in shape and get exercise during their lunch hour or after work.

6e A balanced diet

Writing a formal report

1 Read the report and answer the questions.

  1 What prompted the report to be written?

    _____

  2 What was the main finding?

    _____

  3 What action is proposed?

    _____

Background and aims

There is concern that children at the school are not eating healthily enough, and this is affecting both their general health and their academic performance. In view of this, a short study was commissioned to look into children's diets and make recommendations. The aim of this report is to present those findings and make recommendations.

Findings

Most children are not getting a balanced diet. In the 14–16 age group, only 55 percent of children have school meals. Overall, the lunches provided are a good balance of meat or fish, vegetables, and carbohydrates. However, it is a self-service system and there is no obligation to choose a variety of foods. Accordingly, children tend to choose mainly carbohydrates, especially items like French fries and sweet desserts rather than healthier items.

The remaining 45 bring a packed lunch. The content of these lunches varies greatly—from potato chips and candy to sandwiches and fruit, and apparently, the school makes no specific recommendations on what packed lunches should include.

Recommendations

Although students are given options as to what they can have for lunch, most are making choices that are not balanced; specifically, this means they are eating too much sugar and not enough protein. We recommend that school meals should be compulsory. We also suggest that students be given the choice of different meals, but not a choice of different items within each meal, i.e., they must have a balance of vegetables, protein, and carbohydrates.

2 Find words and phrases in the report with the following meanings but expressed more formally.

  1 Because of this _____

  2 In general _____

  3 But _____

  4 So _____

  5 people say _____

  6 in particular _____

3 **Writing skill avoiding repetition**

a Find these words (1–5) in the report. Then find different ways of expressing the same idea later in the report.

  1 meals _____

  2 balanced diet _____

  3 The content of these lunches

    _____

  4 options _____

  5 We recommend _____

b Express these ideas (1–3) in other words.

  1 The cafeteria staff …

    Those _____

  2 Most children …

    The _____

  3 Hot meals would be good for children

    Hot meals would _____

4 Use the notes below to write a report encouraging schoolchildren to do more sports. Write three paragraphs.

<u>Background and aims</u>
Local school wants to encourage everyone to do sports, not just on school teams.

<u>Main findings</u>
Students sit around at break times; no equipment; not enough P.E. classes.

<u>Recommendations</u>
Organized group early morning exercise; semi-organized sports at break times.

Wordbuilding compound words

1 Circle the correct options to complete these sentences.

1 The movie is about Jim when he's an old man, but it contains a lot of *cutbacks / flashbacks* to his earlier life.

2 The *turnout / turn-up* for the election was over seventy percent this time because many more young people registered to vote.

3 This is probably the most important *break-in / breakthrough* in medical science in thirty years.

4 I sent her a *follow-on / follow-up* letter stressing how interested we are, but I still haven't heard.

5 There's been a complete *breakdown / clampdown* in relations between the two sides—they're not even talking anymore.

6 Try and get a gig at the Beat Café. They're on the *lookalike / lookout* for new talent.

7 She had a kind of *faraway / getaway* look in her eyes.

2 Underline the compound word to complete each definition.

1 A *breakup / getaway* is a quick escape.

2 A *cutback / clampdown* is a reduction in spending.

3 A *turn-up / clampdown* is a severe restriction on activity.

4 A *lookalike / show-off* is a person who is always drawing attention to their achievements.

5 At a *drive-through / drive-about* restaurant, there is no need to get out of your car.

6 A *break-in / breakup* is a separation or disintegration.

Learning skills using phrasal verbs correctly

3 Read the notes below about using phrasal verbs.

1 Often in dictionaries you will find one-word synonyms given for phrasal verbs. These can be misleading. For example: *make up = invent*.

2 Most phrasal verbs are limited in the contexts in which they can be used. You can *make up a story* or *make up an excuse*, for example, but you can't *make up a new product*.

3 So a full definition would be: *make up = invent an account of something*.

4 When you learn a new phrasal verb, you must also learn its limitations before you start to use it.

4 Look at these phrasal verbs and their full definitions, and circle the words that collocate with the phrasal verbs.

1 *call off* = cancel (a scheduled event)

I called off _____ .

a the meeting   c the soccer match

b the hotel reservation   d the wedding

2 *put across* = communicate (one's ideas or feelings)

She put across _____ .

a her proposal   c her decision

b her views   d the news by email

3 *set up* = establish (a new organization or connection)

We set up _____ .

a a good relationship   c a video link

b our own company   d a daily routine

4 *find out* = discover (an answer by consulting or by experience)

I found out _____ .

a an old map   c why she left

b a new car   d the word's meaning

Check!

5 Complete these sentences about exercise and beauty. All the answers are in Student's Book Unit 6.

1 Swogging is a mixture of _____ and _____ .

2 Radio Taiso is a callisthenic exercise routine in _____ .

3 Yoga originated in _____ .

4 Ultrarunning means running _____ distances.

5 Women of the Padaung tribe in Myanmar put copper coils around their _____ to make them longer.

6 People say that beauty is _____ deep (but "ugly" goes clean to the bone)!

7 In Washington State, U.S., fast-food chains have to say how many _____ are in each dish.

8 In 6e, the writer reported on a proposal to make smokers pay more for their _____ .

Unit 7 The digital world

7a The Star Cave

Listening digital exploration

1 Look at the photo of the Star Cave. What do you think the Star Cave is? What does it enable people to do?

2 ▶ 50 Listen to a podcast about Albert Yu-Min Lin and the Star Cave. Answer the questions.

1 What is Lin's job, and how does he do it differently from others in his profession?

_____

_____

2 What is the Star Cave?

_____

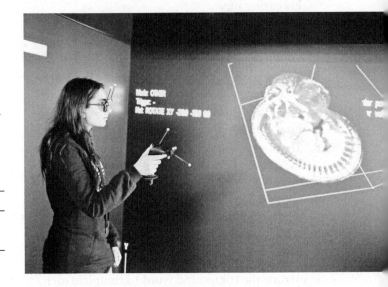

3 ▶ 50 Listen again and circle the correct option (a, b, or c).

1 What are the podcaster's feelings about technology?
   a mixed
   b that it is beneficial on the whole
   c that it creates more problems than it solves

2 What do Lin's digital immersive technologies mean that he can do?
   a He can work from home.
   b He doesn't necessarily have to go into the field to excavate.
   c He can use more sensitive and accurate equipment.

3 What is the tomb of Genghis Khan given as an example of?
   a a place that is deep under the earth
   b a very sensitive subject for local people
   c a place that historians found but never mapped

4 Which of these things is NOT mentioned as something you can do in the Star Cave?
   a survey the landscape as if you were in a plane
   b navigate through underwater cities
   c compare a landscape to past accounts of it

5 What is the future for this type of technology?
   a to be used in biological research
   b to create a complete 3D map of the world
   c to be used in many different disciplines

4 Answer the questions about the words in bold in these phrases from the podcast.

1 ... plastic debris in our oceans is believed to be changing marine ecosystems **irreparably** ...
   Irreparably means it can't be fixed. What root word has _irreparably_ been built from?

2 Lin has **swapped** his spade and trowel for an array of digital 3D immersive technologies.
   What do soccer players swap after a match?

3 What this allows him to do is visualize data using **cutting-edge** tools ...
   Cutting-edge here means "very advanced." What object normally has a cutting edge?

4 ... the tomb is considered to be an extremely **sacred** place ...
   Sacred means it has religious significance to people. Can you think of another word for _sacred_?

5 ... disturbing it could **trigger** a **curse** that would end the world.
   a What triggers a house alarm to go off?
   b Do you think a curse brings good luck or only bad luck?

6 ... the labs where all this data is **crunched** ...
   Crunch literally means "to break up into small pieces, particularly when biting hard on food before swallowing." What does it mean here?

Grammar passive reporting verbs

5 Write these sentences from the podcast using passive reporting verbs.

1 Technology (generally / think / be) a positive thing.
   _____

2 Plastic debris in our oceans (believe / change) marine ecosystems irreparably as we speak.
   _____

3 The quest (know / frustrate) scientists and historians for centuries.
   _____

4 The tomb (consider / be) an extremely sacred place.
   _____

5 Lin learns from an ancient text where a particular mountain (suppose / be) in the past.
   _____

6 These new approaches (expect / benefit) all kinds of projects in the future.
   _____

6 Rewrite these sentences using passive reporting verbs.

1 People think that Lin is unusual because of his varied interests.
   Lin _____
   _____

2 People say that Lin was inspired by an art historian who uses digital imaging.
   Lin _____
   _____

3 We know that Genghis Khan died far from his homeland.
   Genghis Khan _____
   _____

4 People also know that he wanted to be buried in some mountains in the north.
   It _____
   _____

5 We don't expect to find his tomb any time soon.
   His tomb _____

Vocabulary digital media

7 Cross out the incorrect option in each sentence.

1 You can *download / upload / listen to* **music** for free on this website.

2 Feel free to *blog / post / write* **a comment** and tell us what you think.

3 I can use this software to *chat / network / talk* **online** to my parents in Australia.

4 I don't really *go on / tweet / use* **social networking sites**.

5 I look online to see if others have *posted / recommended / reviewed* **a hotel** before I book it.

8 Dictation **photographing Paris**

▶ 51 Listen to this blog post by a photographer in Paris. Complete the blog post.

I was _____
_____
_____ .

I didn't _____ ,
like the Eiffel Tower, _____
_____ .

But _____
_____ ,

instead, I _____
_____ .

So _____ .
They _____
_____
_____ :

more like _____ .

7b Follow us!

Reading exploiting social media

SHAKE WELL.
KEEP REFRIGERATED.
Use within 10 days of opening.
Pasteurized for your protection.

Best Served Cold

FOLLOW US:

PLEASE
RECYCLE

LBF10159

1 Look at these statements about businesses using social media. Do you think the statements are true (T) or false (F)? Then read the article and underline the sentences that provide the evidence for your answers.

1	Many different social media sites are all essentially the same.	T	F
2	Bad use of social media by a company can actually be worse than not using it at all.	T	F
3	Social media has become an integral part of the way companies communicate with customers.	T	F
4	Measuring the success of social media marketing can be done cheaply.	T	F
5	Ideally, your social media marketing will offer customers something they have not seen elsewhere.	T	F
6	The number of people who see your campaign is the most important thing.	T	F

2 Find these words and phrases in the article. Circle the correct meaning (a or b) for each.

1 a minefield
  a something full of unseen risks
  b something certain to end in disaster

2 go about
  a achieve   b approach

3 coherent
  a consistent and logical
  b simple and effective

4 in a roundabout way
  a secretly   b indirectly

Follow us!

For those businesses that are unfamiliar with it, social media marketing can be a minefield. Because there are so many different channels to choose from—YouTube, Instagram, LinkedIn, and Twitter to name just a few—each with a different user profile, it is difficult to know where to begin. And although every business has the same ultimate goal of selling more, each will want to go about this in a different way through its social media campaigns, for example, by trying to attract more visitors to its website or by encouraging interest in a specific product. If you use social media incorrectly, it can actually put customers off; yet not using it is not really an option since it is now a key area in which companies compete with each other for customers' attention. There are, however, some simple principles you can follow to make sure that you are successful.

The first thing is to plan a list of measures that are both achievable and measurable (there are various analytic software tools available at a relatively low cost that monitor both customer traffic and the reaction of those who see your campaign). The second point is to create content that has an equal mix of promotional material, new ideas, and engaging content. Third, it is important to keep your brand identity strong and your message coherent in your social media marketing; just as it is in any other type of advertising that you run. And lastly, as mentioned above, it is vital to choose the right social media channels to reach your target customers. Remember that it is not how many people you reach but whether you reach people with a message that appeals to them.

A good example of a company that has successfully followed these principles is TOMS shoes. TOMS is a social enterprise which, for each pair of shoes it sells, gives a pair of shoes to a child in need. The company asked followers to go without wearing shoes for one day and then post a photo of this on Instagram. They wanted to make people more aware of the millions of children in the world who walk barefoot. The campaign served in a roundabout way to promote TOMS' own "Buy a pair, Give a pair" model. With the help of Instagram, they were able to tell a visual story that their customers could engage with and also gave them immediate feedback on how successful their campaign was.

Grammar nominalization

3 Rewrite the sentences from the article with nominalized forms. Use the prompts in parentheses.

1 Because there are so many different channels to choose from, it is difficult to know where to begin. (wide choice / makes)

_____

_____

2 If you use social media incorrectly, it can actually put customers off. (incorrect use)

_____

_____

3 There are, however, some simple principles you can follow to make sure that you are successful. (ensure / success)

_____

_____

4 Remember that it is not how many people you reach but whether you reach people with a message that appeals to them. (number / matters / appeal)

_____

_____

5 They wanted to make people more aware of the millions of children in the world who walk barefoot. (aim / raise / awareness)

_____

_____

4 Complete the sentences using nominalized forms so that they mean the same as the sentence above.

1 We are not concerned about how much the work costs. It's more important to us that it is done quickly.

Our _____ is not the _____; the _____ is more important.

2 Their advertising campaign did not affect people immediately. It took about three months after they had launched it to become really popular.

The _____ advertising campaign was not immediate. Its _____ came three months after its _____ .

3 Very few people were interested in the sweatshirts at first, but when David Beckham was spotted wearing one, suddenly they started to sell thousands of them.

There was _____ in the sweatshirts initially, but when David Beckham was spotted wearing one, _____ took off.

4 Fewer people booked camping vacations, because summer was very late in arriving.

_____ camping vacations was down owing to the _____ of summer.

Idioms business buzzwords

5 Complete the sentences with these business buzz words.

ballpark	loop	page	practice
reality	rocket	win	

1 I'd say 10,000 is just a _____ figure—who knows what the real potential is?

2 The CEO wants to be kept in the _____ on this project.

3 I don't see how we can go wrong here. It's a _____-win situation.

4 I think our salespeople will understand the product. It's not _____ science.

5 We need to look at examples of best _____ in the industry and follow that model.

6 Are we on the same _____ here? Or do you have different expectations for this initiative?

7 We need a _____ check. Very few people use fax machines anymore.

6 What everyday words and phrases do you think the business buzzwords in bold in these sentences are alternatives for?

1 We've had a few **issues** with our supplier, so we can't send you the goods as promised.

_____

2 Can you **reach out to** the sales team and see who is interested in doing the presentation?

_____

3 We have a lot of talented people working for us, but we're failing to **leverage** that talent.

_____

4 Why would you buy a product for $40 from a store when you can get the same thing online for $25? It's **a no-brainer**.

_____

7c The Cleanweb hackathon

Listening hacking to a brighter future

1 Look at the photo and the heading *hacking to a brighter future*. What do you think a *hackathon* is?

_____

_____

2 ▶ 52 Listen to an interview with a journalist and compare your idea with what the journalist says. What was the focus of the hackathon?

_____

_____

3 ▶ 53 Listen to the first part of the interview and take notes on the following.

1 two alternative expressions for a *hackathon*

_____

2 the typical length of a hackathon

_____

3 three kinds of technology Cleanweb uses to solve environmental problems

_____

4 four areas of environmental improvement that they address

_____

5 what "the resource cloud" was being used to encourage

_____

4 ▶ 54 Listen to the second part of the interview and answer the questions.

1 What did one of the organizers of Cleanweb say we all need to do?

_____

2 What was the atmosphere at the hackathon like?

_____

3 What does the app Econofy allow you to do?

_____

4 What additional reward did the inventors of this app get?

_____

5 In what category would Amrita put Cleanweb?

_____

Word focus *break*

5 Complete the sentences to make expressions with *break*. You have been given the first letter of the missing words.

1 We've already spent $2,500 on new equipment. Another $50 isn't going to **break the b**_____ .

2 So, he's going to have to share an office with four other people. Should I **break the n**_____ to him or will you?

3 I've bitten my nails since I was five years old, and it's very difficult to **break the h**_____ .

4 Thieves **broke i**_____ and stole $10,000 worth of electronic equipment.

5 I always tell a few jokes before I begin a training session to help **break the i**_____ .

6 It's a very difficult piece of translation, but I think I've **broken the b**_____ of it now.

7 We **broke e**_____ in our first year, and this year we'll make a small profit.

7d Sauroniops

Real life making a podcast

1 ▶ 55 Listen to this podcast about a dinosaur find and complete the chart.

What is it?	
Where was it found?	
Who found it?	
What does the discovery tell us about this part of Africa?	

2 Speaking skill hedging language

▶ 55 Complete these statements from the podcast using hedging language. Use one or two words per blank. Then listen again and check your answers.

1 … which _____ to have terrorized North Africa some 95 million years ago.

2 Cau has been able to conclude that this was _____ a large two-legged meat-eater …

3 … and _____ measuring as much as twelve meters in length.

4 The long shape of the skull _____ Sauroniops had a large jaw …

5 The fossil also revealed a large bump on Sauroniops's already thick forehead, from which it _____ this dinosaur used its head in fights …

6 … this area of North Africa _____ have been particularly popular with predatory dinosaurs.

7 Such dinosaurs _____ gather where there was an abundance of food …

8 _____ , says Cau, they targeted different prey and had no need to compete for food.

3 Pronunciation new words

a Look at these words from the podcast. Using what you know about prefixes and suffixes (stress patterns, rules for short or long vowels, etc.), say them as you think they will be pronounced.

abundance
blade
comprise
fossil
geological
jaw
predatory
ripping
skull
two-legged

b ▶ 56 Listen, check, and repeat.

4 Listen and respond historical objects

▶ 57 Imagine you have found an old object of historical interest. Think about what it is, the period it is from, and its significance. Then listen to the questions a friend asks you about it. Answer each question using hedging language. Then compare what you say with the model answer that follows.

1

So what did you find?

It seems to be some kind of old oil lamp.

7e World's smallest

Writing a news report

1 Look at the photo and then read the news report. Underline the parts that answer these questions.

1 Who features in the story?
2 What did the zoologists do?
3 Where did this happen?
4 How did they do it?
5 When did this happen?
6 Why is this important?

Brookesia micra

David Attenborough is one of the world's best-known nature documentary makers, and there are few places on the planet that he has not been and few marvels of nature that he has not seen. So finding the pygmy chameleon on the island of Madagascar half a century after he first began looking for it was very likely a moment of huge personal satisfaction for him.

In 2012, German zoologists found an even smaller species, *Brookesia micra*, on one of the smaller islands off the coast of Madagascar. Attenborough found his pygmy chameleon by looking on the forest floor, where they generally live during the day. The German team used a different method: searching with flashlights at night when the tiny chameleons climb into the trees and are said to be easier to spot.

The discovery is significant because it seems to suggest that in certain circumstances, such as being confined to an island, some animals grow smaller in order to adapt to a restricted habitat. *Brookesia* is almost certainly not the only chameleon to be part of this phenomenon.

2 Writing skill cautious language

a Read the report again and find examples of the following types of cautious language.

a the verb *seem* (para 3)
b a passive reporting verb (para 2)
c an adverb of degree (para 3)
d an adverb of frequency (para 2)
e adverbs that speculate about a fact (paras 1 and 3)

b Make these sentences from the report more cautious using the words in parentheses.

1 David Attenborough is one of the world's best-known nature documentary makers.

_____ (probably)

2 Attenborough found his pygmy chameleon by looking on the forest floor.

_____ (seem)

3 In 2012, German zoologists found an even smaller species.

_____ (apparently)

4 Some animals grow smaller in order to adapt to a restricted habitat.

_____ (believe)

3 Write your own news report using these notes. Write approximately 150 words.

We already know some species of snake can fly.

Some can glide up to 100 meters.

But how?

New study from Virginia Tech has a possible answer.

Snakes flatten their bodies to make a wing.

Heads up, tails down, and glide.

Probably no significance for airplane or military technology.

Wordbuilding verb prefixes

1 Look at the meanings of the verb prefixes below. Then add the correct prefix (*out*, *over*, or *under*) to each verb. (*out* = more than / better than; *over* = too much; *under* = too little)

1 Don't _____**estimate** her. She's a lot more capable than most people think.

2 Statistics show that on average women _____**live** men by approximately three to five years.

3 I think you _____**charged** me for these drinks. It should have come to $12, but you charged $18.

4 There are disadvantages to making children stay at school until they are 18, but these are _____**weighed** by the advantages.

5 I'm amazed he still plays computer games at the age of 45. You would imagine he would have _____**grown** them by now.

6 This chicken is _____**cooked**. It's still pink in the middle.

7 I don't know why you are so angry with him. He was only doing his job. I think you are _____**reacting**.

8 The people in favor of going on were _____**numbered** by those who wanted to turn back.

9 The girls' performance is good, but boys at the school are _____**achieving**. They are capable of much better results.

10 This washing machine _____**performs** its competitors in every aspect: it's quieter, uses less water, cleans better—and it's not that expensive.

Learning skills intensive reading

2 To build your reading speed and ability to comprehend more complex texts, you need to practice intensive reading. Read the notes. Then answer the question.

> Intensive reading is when you read for an accurate and close understanding of the ideas and details in a text. This will often be necessary in work or study.
>
> Which of the following would you do if you were reading intensively?
>
> **a** check new words in a dictionary
>
> **b** skim the text first for a general understanding
>
> **c** try to break down complex sentences into manageable chunks

3 Breaking down text is a key skill with more complex writing. Read this complex sentence and then follow the steps (1–3).

Setting aside for a moment the question of whether you agree with his methods of collecting data or not, the evidence that Jenkins has supplied implies that there is an increase rather than a decrease in the number of people under the age of fifty suffering from memory loss.

1 Identify the main verb, the basic subject of the main verb, and the basic object of that verb.

2 Now define more precisely what the subject and object of the verb are.

3 Finally, look at any subordinate clauses and say what the extra information they give relates to.

4 Follow these steps with other complex sentences in something you have to read in English.

Check!

5 Complete the sentences. Use the first letter of each word to spell a key word from Unit 7a. All the answers are in Student Book Unit 7.

① Unit 7b explains how companies use _____ media to market their products and services.

② If you don't make a profit or a loss, you break _____ .

③ The video in 7f was about saving disappearing _____ .

④ At the DEF CON convention, participants took part in a competition called "Capture the _____ ."

⑤ Artist Liu Bolin is known as "The _____ Man."

⑥ An _____ is a symbol used in messaging, like a smiley face or a sad face.

Word: _____

Unit 8 The music in us

8a Ukulele master

Listening Jake Shimabukuro

1 ▶ 58 Listen to an interview with ukulele player Jake Shimabukuro and answer the questions.

1 When did Shimabukuro start playing?

_____

2 Where are he and his ukulele from?

_____

3 What kind of music did he play at first?

_____

4 What kind of music does he play now?

_____

5 Why does he think everyone should play the ukulele?

_____

_____

2 ▶ 58 Look at these statements. Then listen again and write the word or phrase Shimabukuro uses that has a similar meaning to the phrases in bold. (You can pause each time to give yourself time to write.)

1 When he played the ukulele, Shimabukuro was instantly **addicted**.

_____

2 The ukelele is **Hawaii's traditional instrument**.

_____

3 In high school, there were **small groups of people** with specific interests in music styles.

_____

4 People were **shocked** by his version of "More Than Words."

_____

5 For him, music communicates **powerful feelings**.

_____

6 His grandmother and her friends **enjoy** playing the ukulele.

_____

7 Modern life and modern technology don't give us **time to stop and think**.

_____

3 ▶ 58 Read what Shimabukuro said about the importance of music. Complete the text. Then listen again and check your answers.

> In this day and [1] _____ we live in, where technology always expects us to multitask and give [2] _____ our contemplative time, we're always expected to respond so quickly; it can be [3] _____ . So coming home after a long day, [4] _____ up the ukulele, and playing it feels like a [5] _____ session to me! It gives you the chance to let loose and act [6] _____ !

4 Match these words (1–5) from the interview with their definitions (a–e).

1 recorder ____   a a melody
2 chord ____   b a version of someone
3 tune ____   else's composition
4 note ____   c a single musical tone
5 cover song   d a wind instrument
   ____   e a group of single musical
                     tones played together

Grammar the adverb *just*

5 Replace the words in bold in these sentences with *just* and write it in the correct position in the sentence.

1 We got back from our trip **very recently**.
2 The new museum is **simply** stunning.
3 That's what I think **exactly**.
4 We **only** use bicycles; we don't own a car.
5 There are **a little** under three million people living in the city.

6 Write *just* in the correct place in the numbered lines.

One of the song titles on Shimabukuro's album *Peace, Love and Ukulele* consists
1 of three numbers: 143. Shimabukuro says that the song was written for his fiancée at the time and that the significance is that
2 in those days they had pagers, not cell phones. 143 means "I love you" in numeric code. So he used to page her with that code,
3 in the same way that some people now text the letters *ILY*. Even after pagers were replaced with cell phones, they still used
4 the code because it was something they
5 both understood. So the song is a piece of nostalgia, really.

7 Look at the pairs of sentences. Then choose the correct meaning of *just* (a, b, or c) for each sentence.

1 I remember playing "More Than Words" by Extreme, and everyone just freaked out! _____
   I just remember playing "More Than Words" by Extreme, and everyone freaked out! _____
   a simply   b exactly   c only

2 It's a more intimate connection than just having a conversation with someone. _____
   It's taken just over two years to build up that more intimate connection. _____
   a very recently   b a little   c only

3 My grandmother has just started playing it. _____
   Just my grandmother started playing it. _____
   a exactly   b recently   c only

4 ... just taking that step to give any kind of instrument a try will bring people immense joy. _____
   ... taking that step to give any kind of instrument a try is just the right thing to do. _____
   a simply   b exactly   c a little

8 Pronunciation expressions with *just*

a ▶ 59 Match the questions (1–5) with the correct responses (a–e). Then listen and check.

1 Should we go? _____
2 How are you doing? _____
3 Can I help you? _____
4 Why do you ask? _____
5 Is Jaz there? _____

a No, thanks. I'm just looking.
b I'm just curious.
c No. He just left.
d Yes, I'm just coming.
e Just fine, thanks.

b ▶ 59 Now listen again to the questions. Pause so that you can respond yourself.

Vocabulary extra music

9 Write these words in the appropriate categories in the chart.

eclectic   folk   hum
naturally gifted   pianist   upbeat

Genres of music	_____ _____
Moods of music	_____ _____ _____
Types of musician	_____ _____
Ways of singing	_____
Tastes in music	_____ _____
Attributes of a musician	_____ _____

10 Read the conversation. Then put the words in bold in the correct category in the chart in Exercise 9.

A: I saw John Williams in concert last night. You know, the **composer** and guitarist?
B: Yes, he's very **accomplished**. I've heard some of the stuff he did with Segovia: it's very **expressive** — and **romantic**, too.
A: Yes, it is. Last night he surprised us with some West African pieces. I'm not sure the audience, which was pretty **conservative**, enjoyed it that much. I think they were expecting him to play his better-known **classical** compositions.

8b Music therapy

Reading active and passive

1 What do you know about music therapy? What kinds of conditions do you think that music therapy would be helpful in treating? Read the article and make a list of the conditions it mentions.

_____

_____

2 Read the article again. Are these sentences true (T) or false (F)?

1 The stereotypical view of music therapy is completely wrong.   T   F

2 Active music therapy stimulates parts of the brain that are not functioning properly.   T   F

3 Passive music therapy is used to help learning as well as for relaxation.   T   F

4 The "Mozart Effect" helps patients sleep.   T   F

5 Many people know that music can have an uplifting effect.   T   F

6 The Cochrane research means that fewer drugs may be used in the future to treat depression.   T   F

Music therapy

A stereotypical image of music therapy is a sing-a-long at a nursing home organized to alleviate boredom or to stimulate nostalgic memories of days gone by. But like all stereotypes, while founded on an element of truth, it is such a simplified view that it does not give anything like a complete picture of music therapy's potential to heal.

There are essentially two types of music therapy: active and passive. Active music therapy includes composing lyrics or music, playing instruments, chanting or choral singing, exercising to music, and dance. The principle is to get participants actively involved so that they will use parts of their brains and bodies that would otherwise be disengaged. Active therapy is proven to be highly effective in the treatment of Alzheimer's, dementia, multiple sclerosis, and Parkinson's.

Passive music therapy, as the name suggests, involves a more relaxing type of participation, usually simple listening exercises. The idea here is to use music in order to make the subject feel less stressed. So passive therapy can be effective in reducing anxiety and blood pressure, lessening post-operative pain, but also it can also be used for improvement of concentration and memory.

There is now so much research into this field that new applications for music therapy are being found all the time. In a Slovak hospital, newborn babies are played classical music through headphones for twenty minutes at a time. Doctors believe that helps them to feel less stressed after birth and to remain healthy at a critical time, as most of them either fall asleep or lie quietly while the music is being played. This seems to agree with the "Mozart Effect" reported some years ago in _Nature_ magazine, which showed that listening to a Mozart piano sonata for ten minutes prior to taking an intelligence test improved students' scores.

In another study by the Cochrane Collaboration, music therapy was found to benefit people suffering from depression. A lot of us use music to lift our spirits or at least are aware of its potential to do that, but up to now, this had not been clinically proven. Doctors have for a long time been looking for alternative therapies to avoid being so dependent on drugs to treat depression, and the Cochrane research offers real hope in this area.

Grammar purpose and result

3 Read these excerpts from the article. Then rewrite the phrases in bold using the words in parentheses.

1 It is **such a simplified** view that it does not give anything like a complete picture. (so)
This view _____ that it does not give anything like a complete picture.

2 The principle is to get participants actively involved **so that they will use** parts of their brains and bodies that would otherwise be disengaged. (so as to)
The principle is to get participants actively involved _____ parts of their brains and bodies that would otherwise be disengaged.

3 The idea here is to use music **in order to make the subject feel less** stressed. (to prevent)
The idea here is to use music _____ _____ stressed.

4 It can also be used **for improvement of** concentration and memory. (to)
It can also be used _____ concentration and memory.

5 A lot of us use music **to lift our spirits**. (because)
A lot of us use music _____ our spirits.

6 Doctors have been looking for alternative therapies **to avoid being** so dependent on drugs. (so as not to)
Doctors have been looking for alternative therapies _____ so dependent on drugs.

4 Match the actions (1–5) with the reasons for doing them (a–e) and use the reasons to write the correct expression of purpose to connect the two parts.

1 He left his job at the bank
_____

2 We perform live sometimes, but just
_____

3 Please turn off any phones or music devices
_____

4 You have to practice
_____

5 Singers drink a lot of water
_____

a fun.
b avoid getting throat problems.
c get better.
d concentrate on playing music.
e disturb other passengers.

Idioms music

5 Complete these idioms. You have been given the first letter of the missing words.

1 Let's not go in with a particular strategy. Let's just **p_____ it by ear**.

2 I don't know why she **made** such **a big song and d_____ about** having to stay late.

3 **You've changed your t_____** . Yesterday you said you really wanted to go.

4 The news was **music to my e_____** .

5 I don't mean to **blow my own h_____** , but I think that went pretty well.

6 What he said about the importance of hard work really **struck a c_____** with me.

7 OK. It's time to **f_____ the music**. I hope she's not too angry.

6 Dictation learn fast

▶ 60 Listen to this advice about learning a musical instrument. Complete the paragraph.

Is there _____ ?
What _____ ?
The answer _____
_____ .
To _____ .
You can _____ ,
_____ .
You may _____ ,
_____ .
I always _____ :
_____ ;
practice — _____
_____ ; and _____ .
Progress _____
_____
_____ .

8c Delta blues

Listening Sonny Boy Williamson II

1 ▶ 61 You are going to listen to an account of the life of blues musician Sonny Boy Williamson II. Look at the photo and then listen and answer the questions.

1 What instrument did he play?

_____

2 What kind of character was he?

_____

3 How is he remembered today?

_____

jamming (v) /'dʒæmiŋ/ playing with other musicians
acclaim (n) /ə'kleɪm/ applause, approval
aficionado (n) /ə,fɪʃiə'nɑːdəʊ/ an enthusiastic follower, a fan

2 ▶ 61 Listen again and circle the best answer (a, b, or c) for each question.

1 Why is it surprising that so few people have heard of Sonny Boy Williamson II?
   a He was very famous in his own lifetime.
   b His music is often played on the radio.
   c He was a very original musician.

2 What do we know about his early life?
   a nothing
   b that he worked on a plantation
   c that he probably had a tough life

3 Which of these describes Sonny Boy's life in the 1930s to the 1950s?
   a a family man
   b a wanderer
   c a man with a mission

4 What is it that sets Sonny Boy apart from other musicians?
   a his individuality and charisma
   b the consistency of his playing
   c the truthfulness of his lyrics

5 How did Jimmy Page feel after his encounter with Sonny Boy?
   a upset with him
   b grateful to him
   c admiring of him

6 Which of these statements about Sonny Boy's death is true?
   a It came at a point in his career when he was playing his best.
   b He was seventy when he died.
   c He was in good shape for his age.

3 ▶ 61 Complete this account of Sonny Boy Williamson's life. Then listen again and check.

Sonny Boy Williamson II was perhaps the first black media [1] _____ of the American South. His [2] _____ show in the early 1940s was very popular in and around Helena, Arkansas. Sonny Boy grew up in [3] _____ times and started playing the blues harp when he was [4] _____ . He had a trick where he could play without using his [5] _____ . He spent his early career [6] _____ around the South, jamming with other musicians.

His music combines [7] _____ rhythms with powerful solos, and although he sounds weary, there is no [8] _____ in his songs. Above all, Sonny Boy had great [9] _____ .

In the 1960s, he toured [10] _____ and met young musicians who became [11] _____ by his music. He loved the [12] _____ he was given. Sonny Boy died in 1965 when he was still at the peak of his powers.

Word focus *hit*

4 Complete the sentences using expressions with *hit*.

miss   nerve   real   record   nail

1 You've **hit the** _____ **on the head**.
2 It's a bit of a **hit-or-** _____ approach.
3 Did I **hit a** _____ when I said that?
4 This app is a _____ **hit** with musicians.
5 "Born Blind" wasn't his first **hit** _____ .

8d Desert Island Discs

Real life your favorite music

1 ▶ 62 Listen to a "castaway" talking about her life and music. Answer the questions.

1 What is Aleah's family background?

_____

2 What do you think her profession is?

_____

3 How did her parents influence her choice of career?

_____

2 Speaking skill responding to questions

▶ 62 Complete the phrases that Aleah gave when she needed time to think before responding. Use between two and four words per blank. Then listen again and check.

1 "Was it obvious to you that you'd go into music as a profession?"

"No, I never _____ like that."

2 "Why?"

"That's a _____ ."

3 "The settled life she never had, maybe?"

"I _____ know. But I don't think so."

4 "Was it the pull of the music world that made you leave?"

"Hmm, _____ say. I don't think it was as simple …"

5 "And so you took off to India. Were your parents unhappy about that?"

"Do you know, I couldn't _____ ."

3 Pronunciation intonation to express uncertainty

a ▶ 63 Look at this list of phrases and check (✓) the ones you expect to be pronounced with an uncertain or wavering intonation. Then listen and check.

1 I'm not sure. ☐
2 I have no idea. ☐
3 Perhaps. ☐
4 It could be. ☐
5 Of course. ☐
6 I doubt it. ☐

b Practice answering these questions. Use the uncertain answers from Exercise 3a with a wavering intonation.

1 Are these the final figures?
2 Is it cheaper to take the bus?
3 Are you coming to the party on Friday?
4 Is the bank open on Saturdays?

4 Listen and respond responding to difficult questions

▶ 64 Listen to someone asking you questions about your background and your music preferences. Respond with your own words. Then compare your response with the model answer that follows.

1 *Did music play a big part in your childhood?*

That's a good question. Certainly it was important in high school. Your circle of friends tended to be influenced a lot by the kind of music you listened to.

8e Filmi

Writing a description

1 Read the description of a style of music from India called *filmi* and answer the questions.

  1 Who sings these songs, and where can you hear them?

      _____

  2 Does the writer recommend listening to this type of music?

      _____

      _____

2 Read the description again and find examples of the following:

  1 two powerful adjectives (para 1)

      _____

  2 a simile—a comparison using *like* or *as* (para 1)

      _____

  3 a description of the atmosphere (para 1)

      _____

  4 a description of how the listener feels listening to this music (para 3)

      _____

  5 the writer speaking directly to the reader (para 3)

      _____

  6 two parallel structures (paras 2 and 3)

      _____

3 Writing skill parallel structures

Complete these parallel structures using your own words. Make sure that the elements of each half of the sentence balance.

  1 Wherever you go in India, you are greeted with warm smiles and _____ .

  2 The songs are not only rich in Hindi folk tradition, but also _____ .

  3 *Filmi* songs vary in type. Some are gentle ballads, others _____ .

  4 *Filmi* represents both India's traditional side _____ .

  5 On a visit to the Bollywood studios, I was captivated by the performance of the actors and actresses: singing along to the music, _____ , and _____ .

  6 While most movie studios make a variety of movie types, Bollywood _____ .

Produced in the thousands every year, *filmi* songs are a genre unlike any other. Go nearly anywhere in India and you will be accompanied by the latest *filmi* hit blaring out from radios in taxicabs and roadside vendors' stalls. The songs fill the air like a throng of happy voices adding to the already hectic nature of Indian city life, an environment that threatens to overwhelm your senses with its vibrant colors, rich smells, and deafening traffic.

Filmi are essentially movie soundtrack songs. In mass-market Indian movies, the action is frequently interrupted by spectacular song-and-dance sequences, in which the actors lip-sync music sung by Indian pop stars. It's a simple commercial formula: match the prettiest faces on screen with the best voices around. The best-known *filmi* come from the Bollywood movie industry. "Bollywood," based in Mumbai, is the Los Angeles of India.

The music, a fusion of traditional Hindu folk music and a variety of other Western styles such as pop and hip hop, is joyous and infectious. You can't help tapping your foot along to the rhythm. It's not great music; it's feel-good music, made to be danced to, both on and off the screen. It's not really my kind of music, and it may not be yours. But I'd be surprised if you weren't carried along in its happy wake.

Wordbuilding onomatopoeic words

1 The word *hum*—as in to "hum a tune"—is an onomatopoeic word; in other words, it sounds like the action itself. Try to match these other onomatopoeic verbs with the correct noun or phrase.

1	beep	○	○	your head
2	bump	○	○	a guitar
3	clap	○	○	a balloon
4	gulp	○	○	the horn
5	mumble	○	○	your hands
6	pop	○	○	with boredom
7	sigh	○	○	on the window
8	strum	○	○	with relief
9	tap	○	○	the words
10	yawn	○	○	down a drink

2 Complete the sentences using the correct form of five of the verbs from Exercise 1.

1 "I don't think I'll ever have an opportunity like that again," she _____ .

2 She continued to _____ her gum even after I asked her to stop.

3 Sorry, I can't understand what you're saying. You're _____ .

4 He _____ lightly on the door so as not to disturb the neighbors.

5 I think when I _____ he thought I was tired of his company, but actually I was just tired from lack of sleep.

Learning skills pronunciation

3 Use your dictionary to check the pronunciation of new words. You will need to do the following:

a recognize the phonetic symbols in this chart.

b note where the stress comes: after the stress mark ('), e.g., *interest* /'ɪntrest/.

iː peace	ɪ hit	ʊ could	uː school	ɪə here	eɪ play	
e hen	ə Africa	ɜː(r) bird	ɔː ball	ʊə(r) pure	ɔɪ boy	əʊ note
æ man	ʌ but	ɑː(r) start	ɒ not	eə(r) where	aɪ like	aʊ now

p pen	b band	t ten	d dance	tʃ change	dʒ just	k can	g go
f fun	v very	θ thing	ð the	s song	z zoo	ʃ she	ʒ visual
m miss	n no	ŋ sing	h his	l like	r red	w west	j you

4 Look at these words related to different music styles written in phonetic script. Say what the word is and where the stress is.

Example:

/'klæsɪkəl/ = clas<u>si</u>cal

1 /'reɡeɪ/ _____

2 /'kʌntrɪ/ _____

3 /kə'lɪpsəʊ/ _____

4 /ɪkspərə'mentl/ _____

5 /'fjuːʒən/ _____

6 /'ɒprə/ _____

Check!

5 Can you remember the following from Student's Book Unit 8?

1 Two words for musicians:

a a _____ = an artist who plays by himself/herself

b a _____ = a group of musicians

2 Two musical words used in expressions:

a change your _____ = to give a different opinion from your original one

b strike a _____ = to say something that elicits a positive (emotional) response

3 Two words beginning with *f*:

a _____ = a melancholy style of song native to Portugal

b _____ the music = accept criticisms for something you have done

4 Two similar-sounding words:

a an _____ guitar = the opposite of an acoustic guitar

b _____ tastes = an interest in a variety of kinds of music

5 The word that sums up Bob Marley's message of unity to the world and completes the name of one of his songs:

"One _____"

Unit 9 Window on the past

9a Letter to yourself

Listening a writing project

1 ▶ 65 Listen to a news report and answer the questions.

1 Who wrote letters to themselves? _____

2 What did the letters contain?
_____

3 In what way have they become "historical documents"? _____

2 ▶ 65 Listen again and answer the questions.

1 What did Farrer's students think his reasons were for giving them this assignment?
_____

2 What did Farrer do with each letter?
_____

3 What does he mainly want his students to do with the letters?
_____

4 What two things make returning the letters worthwhile?
_____

5 What choice did he give to students writing the letters?
_____

6 Why did the boy dream of marrying a Swedish girl?
_____

7 What adjectives sum up Farrer's character?
_____

3 Use these words to complete the phrases you heard in the report. Use the definitions in parentheses to help.

distinct	fulfill	profound
straightforward	through	track

1 a _____ purpose (clear and definite)
2 see the job _____ (complete)
3 be on the right _____ (follow a good path)
4 a _____ job (simple)
5 _____ one's wish (achieve one's goal)
6 _____ effect (deep impact)

Vocabulary extra prepositional phrases related to time

4 Complete the prepositional phrases in bold using these prepositions.

at   back   from   in   in   to

1 _____ **time**, Farrer hopes that his students will come to appreciate what he did. _____

2 _____ **the outset**, it was always Farrer's intention to send the letters back to his students. _____

3 He responded to them **one _____ a time**. _____

4 _____ **retrospect**, Farrer feels that he should have told them what he was going to do. _____

5 _____ **in the days** when Farrer was a child, letter writing was a much more common thing. _____

6 _____ **date**, he has sent over 1,000 letters back to former students. _____

5 Match the bold phrases from Exercise 4 (1–6) with each of these meanings (a–f).

a looking back
b up to now
c from the beginning
d individually
e eventually
f at a time in the past

Grammar linking words

6 Rewrite the sentences or pairs of sentences using the words in bold.

1 After they had handed them in, they forgot about them. **... and, subsequently...**

_____

2 Although he retired fully from teaching in 2006, Farrer kept all the letters carefully filed. **In spite of ...**

_____

3 After he retired, he continued mailing the letters back to his former students. **Following ...**

_____

4 The exercise is greatly valued by his past students, partly because letters are rarer and more precious nowadays. **... partly owing to ...**

_____

5 Not all the students agreed for him to read their letters, but he has kept and is returning these letters, too. **... Nevertheless ...**

_____

7 Rewrite these sentences or pairs of sentences using appropriate linking words or phrases of reason, contrast, and addition as indicated. There is sometimes more than one option.

1 Some students were too embarrassed to make their letters public. Their letters were immature. (reason)

_____

2 The exercise has had a profound effect on the students. Farrer remains modest about his part in its success. (contrast)

_____

3 Farrer thought the idea would inspire his students to write more. He also hoped they would think more about the importance of education in their lives. (addition)

_____

4 Another student wrote that he wanted to go to college and play soccer. He graduated from high school and went to work in a steel mill. (contrast / sequence)

_____

Vocabulary examining evidence

8 Complete the conversation using these words.

clues   deduced   determined
evidence   indicated   uncovered

A: I hear that they've [1] _____ an old Viking ship on the banks of the Thames River.

B: Yes, that's right. They haven't actually [2] _____ exactly what kind of ship it was, but some of the [3] _____ they've found has [4] _____ that it might have been a burial ship.

A: What does that mean?

B: It's when someone important was buried at sea. Their body was usually cremated and then placed on a boat with some of their possessions and put out to sea.

A: And were there any [5] _____ as to who this person was?

B: Not really, but because of the size of ship, they have [6] _____ that it must have been someone very important.

9 Dictation gladiator school

▶ 66 Listen to this description of an archeological find in Austria. Complete the paragraph.

Archeologists _____

_____

_____

_____

_____ Colosseum.

The facility _____

_____

_____

_____

_____ .

In addition _____ .

_____

_____

_____

_____

_____ .

9b Three famous fraudsters

Reading notorious con artists

1 Read the description of three con artists. Write down their crimes and what punishment, if any, they received.

William Thompson
Crime(s): _____
Punishment: _____

Natwarlal
Crime(s): _____
Punishment: _____

Ferdinand Demara
Crime(s): _____
Punishment: _____

2 Read the article again and answer the questions.

1 In what way was William Thompson a fake?

_____

2 What is the phrase meaning "to trust someone" that William Thompson became known for?

_____

3 What is meant by the phrase *a master of disguises* to describe Natwarlal?

_____

4 What does the writer suggest happened to Natwarlal in the end?

_____

5 What two things helped make Ferdinand Demara a successful impersonator?

_____

6 Why did his career in impersonating decline?

_____

Three famous fraudsters

William Thompson was a small-time fraudster who was active in New York City in the 1840s. His main claim to fame is that he is said to be responsible for the coining of the term "confidence trickster" ⁵ or "con artist." Preying on upper-class citizens, he would engage them in polite conversation and at a certain point ask if they "had confidence in him" to lend him their watch or some money until the following day. Believing him to be a gentleman ¹⁰ (Thompson was always well-dressed and well-spoken), they would generally hand over the watch or money, never to see it again. He was arrested and put on trial in 1849 and subsequently sent to prison.

Mithilesh Kumar Srivastava, known as Natwarlal, ¹⁵ was an Indian con man who was arrested nine times in his life and sentenced to a total of 113 years in prison for his crimes. Considering that he had been charged with over eighty crimes of fraud and forgery, the length of these sentences is ²⁰ not surprising. He was an expert forger and also a master of disguises, but the frauds for which he is best known are those where he "sold" various famous buildings, including the Taj Mahal, to tourists. On every occasion that he was caught, ²⁵ Natwarlal managed to escape again. He was last arrested in 1996 when he was 84 and, having given the police the slip at Delhi station on his way to prison, was never seen again, and presumably now never will be.

³⁰ Ferdinand Waldo Demara Jr. was known as "The Great Impostor." During his life, he impersonated a monk, an editor, a lawyer, a child-care expert, and a psychologist, among other things. He claimed that the secret of his success was finding roles to fill ³⁵ that did not threaten other people's positions in an organization. Also, compared to other impersonators, Demara was unusual in that he seems not to have been interested in money. Having published the story of his exploits in the 1950s, Demara became quite a ⁴⁰ well-known figure in the U.S., making it difficult for him to carry out further impersonations. Knowledge of his past also discouraged employers from giving him work, despite the fact that he was a highly intelligent man. After a long period of time in the ⁴⁵ hospital, he died in 1982.

3 Look at these expressions from the article and circle the correct definition (a or b).

1 preying on (line 5)
   a circulating among   b targeting as victims
2 put on trial (line 13)
   a convicted b prosecuted
3 give someone the slip (line 26–27)
   a escape capture   b cheat someone
4 exploits (line 39)
   a crimes b adventures

Grammar **present and perfect participles**

4 Look at how the seven participles listed below are used in the article. Is the subject of each participle the same as the subject of the main verb? If so, who or what is that subject?

Participle

1 Preying   (line 5) *Same   Thompson (he)*
2 Believing (line 9) _____
3 Considering (line 17) _____
4 having given (line 26) _____
5 compared to (line 36) _____
6 Having published (line 38) _____
7 making (line 40) _____

5 Complete the sentences using the correct participle form of the verb in parentheses.

1 _____ their trust, he then persuaded his victims to lend him money. (gain)
2 _____ the con artist displays a casual, good-humored attitude, most people are usually fooled. (provide)
3 _____ bank drafts that he had forged, Natwarlal defrauded banks and jewelers of huge amounts of money. (use)
4 _____ that most bank transactions these days are done with pin numbers and passwords, Natwarlal's methods would not be so effective now. (give)
5 _____ that he must be dead by now, the authorities have given up looking for him. (assume)
6 _____ from his victims' point of view, Natwarlal's arrests were little comfort, as the money he stole was never found. (see)

7 While impersonating a ship's surgeon, Demara, _____ up about what he needed to do, performed successful surgery on a wounded soldier. (read)
8 _____ he was so intelligent and also that he had a photographic memory, Demara could easily have found a good job as himself. (consider)

6 Combine each pair of sentences using participles. You will need to change, add, or delete some words.

1 She tried a few times. Then she gave up.
   _____

2 I stood in front of the White House. I was amazed at how much smaller it is compared to how it looks on TV.
   _____

3 He's so young. It's not fair to ask him to practice the piano for four hours a day.
   _____

4 She feared she would be the first to arrive. So she walked around the block a few times.
   _____

5 Can I assume you're happy with the arrangements? If so, I'll send out the invitations.
   _____

Vocabulary **crime and punishment**

7 Complete this passage using one word in each blank.

Jaime was caught on camera driving in a bike lane downtown. Two weeks later, he received a letter ordering him to appear in [1]_____ . He was [2]_____ with reckless driving. Jaime said that he was not [3]_____ , claiming that he had moved into the bike lane to let an ambulance pass. The case was [4]_____ before a judge, and Jaime was [5]_____ guilty and ordered to pay a [6]_____ of $500. He appealed the conviction.

9c Mutiny on the *Bounty*

Listening trouble in paradise

1 ▶ 67 You are going to listen to a story about a mutiny. Read the definition. Then listen to the story and answer the questions.

mutiny (n) /ˈmjuː.tə.ni/ unlawful refusal to obey one's commander or the authorities, especially rebellion by sailors against their superior officers

1 When and where did this mutiny happen?
_____

2 What was the motive for the mutiny?
_____

3 Did the story end happily, or not?
_____

2 ▶ 67 Listen again and answer these questions.

1 What was the reason for the ship's voyage?
_____

2 What became of the captain and the crew that was loyal to him?
_____

3 Who was in the group that landed at Pitcairn Island with Christian to start a new life?
_____

4 What did Christian do to the *Bounty* after he arrived at Pitcairn?
_____

5 What became of the mutineers in Tahiti?
_____

6 What was the cause of the dispute between the Tahitians and the mutineers on Pitcairn?
_____

7 What became of Fletcher Christian himself?
_____

3 Answer the questions about the words in bold in these sentences from the story.

1 … one of the most **atrocious** acts of piracy …
Did Captain Bligh see this as a "daring" act or a "terrible" act?
_____

2 In a boat only seven meters long, heavily **laden** with nineteen men …
What word that is similar to *laden* could you put here? _____

3 Christian had **stripped** the *Bounty* …
What things do you think he took off the boat?
_____

4 Christian knew the English Admiralty **had a long arm** …
What does this phrase suggest that Christian feared? _____

4 Complete the summary of the story.

In 1787, the *Bounty* [1] _____ from Spithead in England on its way to Tahiti to collect [2] _____ to take to the West Indies. After six months in Tahiti, the acting mate led a [3] _____ against the [4] _____ , William Bligh. They put him and some of his crew in a [5] _____ and cast him adrift in the [6] _____ . Miraculously, Bligh managed to survive and [7] _____ to England. Some of Christian Fletcher's crew stayed in Tahiti, but Christian himself, with eight crew and eighteen [8] _____ , journeyed on to [9] _____ , a small [10] _____ island. Here, he [11] _____ the ship. Following arguments between the [12] _____ and the [13] _____ , fighting broke out, resulting in the deaths of all but [14] _____ of the original crew.

Word focus *board*

5 Underline the correct words to complete these idioms.

1 We need to **go back to the** *drawing board / planning sheet* here. Our plan isn't working.

2 There will be a three percent pay increase *across / throughout* **the board**. Managers will get the same raise as other employees.

3 I'll try to *bring / take* everyone's **views on board,** but I can't promise that everyone will be happy with the solution we come up with.

4 He's offering to sell you a brand new bike at half its normal price. Are you sure it's all *above / on* **board**?

5 It's just a casual party. I think spending $100 on an outfit **is going** *outboard / overboard*.

9d I'll give you an example

Real life checking, confirming, and clarifying

1 ▶ 68 Listen to a conversation about a lecture on table manners. Are the statements true (T) or false (F) about table manners in the Middle Ages?

1 People didn't wipe their hands or mouths after eating.   T   F

2 People helped themselves to whatever food was on the table.   T   F

3 It was normal for people to spit sometimes during a meal.   T   F

4 The use of forks came after spoons and knives.   T   F

5 The main speaker thinks that table manners have definitely improved since then.   T   F

2 ▶ 68 Complete the phrases for checking, confirming, and clarifying information. Then listen again and check your answers.

1 What do you _____ _____ "etiquette"? Like table manners?

2 _____ you _____ that they didn't really have food served up on individual plates?

3 So, in _____ _____ , it was a bit of a free-for-all.

4 By today's standards it *would* seem very rude, but _____ _____ is that politeness is a relative thing.

5 Am I _____ _____ thinking that forks came a bit later?

6 _____ I _____ was that that's when we can see the beginning of modern table manners.

3 Which phrases in Exercise 2:
a) check meaning?

_____

b) clarify meaning?

_____

4 Pronunciation silent letters

a ▶ 69 Look at these words and underline the letters that are not pronounced. Then listen and check.

island
handkerchief
foreign
honor
salmon
castle
subtle
guesthouse
whoever
wrap
psychiatrist
Wednesday

b ▶ 69 Listen again and practice saying the words in Exercise 4a.

5 Listen and respond checking facts

▶ 70 Imagine you are talking to a friend who has seen a TV program about the modern world of technology. Listen to each fact. Use the information to make a question or to ask for confirmation or clarification of what you have heard. Then compare what you say with the model answer that follows.

1

> *I saw a great program last night about the making of the modern world.*

> *What do you mean by "the making of" the modern world?*

9e The folly of war

Writing describing a past event

1 Read the essay about the Charge of the Light Brigade and answer the questions.

1 What was the result of this cavalry charge?

_____

2 How does the writer express a view about this event?

_____

The Charge of the Light Brigade took place during the battle of Balaclava in 1854 between a joint British–French–Turkish force and the Russian army. The British and French were positioned to the west of a valley with the main Russian army and their guns facing them at the other end in the east. The Russians had some hours earlier captured British guns on hills on the south side of the valley in fortified positions called redoubts.

Viewing the scene from a hill behind the British lines, Lord Raglan ordered the British cavalry to attack the redoubts on the south side. He gave this order to Captain Nolan who rode down into the valley to pass it on to the commander of the cavalry, Lord Lucan. Lucan, who did not have the advantage of being able to see the situation from a high vantage point, asked what guns were to be attacked. Nolan mistakenly indicated the guns at the eastern end of the valley.

Accordingly, 600 cavalrymen set off down the valley straight for the main Russian force with guns firing at them from all sides. Approximately 200 returned. The following day, a French marshal, Bosquet, said of the action: "It is magnificent, but it is not war; it is madness."

2 Underline two time phrases in the article that do the following:

a indicate a time before the main event (para 1)

b tell you about an event that happened after the main event (para 3)

3 Writing skill **sequencing events**

Read the first sentence in each pair. Complete the reported version with a past time phrase.

1 He is working for a bank at the moment.
He was working for a bank _____ .

2 She arrived a few days ago.
She had arrived _____ .

3 Up to now, no one has heard of airplanes.
_____ , no one had heard of airplanes.

4 The election takes place tomorrow.
The election took place _____ .

5 Last year, there was a bad storm.
_____ , there had been a bad storm.

4 In 1937, the Hindenburg airship exploded while docking in New Jersey. Use these notes to write an account of an amazing escape from the Hindenburg.

Hindenburg airship passes over Boston, morning May 6th, 1937.

Hindenburg left Germany for US May 3rd.

Bad weather delays landing at Lakehurst, New Jersey

Cabin boy Werner Franz works in kitchen on Hindenburg

He plans to visit New York before Hindenburg returns to Germany May 7th

The captain is trying to steer the airship next to a docking tower

There is a loud bang, and Franz sees a big ball of flame

The skin of the ship has broken; hydrogen inside has ignited

Ship crashes to the ground. Onlookers run for their lives.

Franz opens the kitchen hatch where food is pulled up into the kitchen and jumps

He runs to safety

Ten minutes after the fire starts, there is nothing left of the airship

Wordbuilding verb + preposition

1 Put these verbs in the correct group according to the prepositions that follow them.

account adjust base   benefit   count
long   resign result specialize subscribe

1 _____
  _____ } on
  insist

4 _____
  succeed   } in
  _____

2 _____
  pay   } for
  _____

5 _____
  recover   } from
  _____

3 _____
  refer   } to
  _____

2 Complete the sentences using the correct verb and preposition combinations from Exercise 1.

1 Don't worry. You can _____ _____ me.

2 It took a while to _____ _____ living in a new country, but I love it now.

3 How do you _____ _____ the fact that married men live longer than single men?

4 She didn't _____ _____ her job; she was forced out!

5 I _____ _____ the day when people can live together in peace.

6 I suspect the cuts will _____ _____ a lot of people losing their jobs.

Learning skills revising in writing

3 In your Student Book, various models are presented for different types of writing, and it is always useful to follow a basic structure for each type of writing. Bear in mind, however, the following points about the act of writing:

1 Writing is not always a linear process of planning, drafting, and revising. Everyone composes their writing in a different way.

2 Your ideas will develop as you write, so you don't have to stick to a predetermined plan.

3 It's natural to rethink and revise your ideas while you are writing.

4 Wait until the end to check the grammar or sentence structure, or you will interrupt the flow of your thoughts.

5 Remember that the best writing is economical. So, when rereading at the end, pay attention to what seems unnecessary—and cut it!

4 Think about a piece of writing you have done in this course and how you approached it. How true are the points in Exercise 3 for you?

Check!

5 Look at the photos from Unit 9 in the Student Book and complete the summaries of stories relating to each photo.

1 Archeologists say: "It's not what you _____ that matters; it's what you find _____ ." The Stones of Stenness are _____ of a sophisticated society, while other objects that were uncovered give valuable _____ to this being a rich trading community.

2 W.E.B. Dubois was an American sociologist and civil _____ activist. He sent his daughter to school in England and, shortly _____ , sent her a letter telling her not to shrink _____ new experiences and to remember that her father believed _____ her.

3 Arnaud de Tilh was an _____ who pretended to be another man, Martin Guerre, in order to _____ his estate. He was accused _____ fraud, taken to court, and _____ guilty.

4 The *Bom Jesus* was a Portuguese ship carrying _____ to India to trade in exchange for _____ . It was blown off course and _____ off the _____ of Namibia.

Unit 10 Social living

10a Social animals

Listening the thoughtful elephant

1 ▶ 71 Look at the title and the photo below. Then listen to an interview with a naturalist and circle the adjectives that match her description of female elephant behavior.

aggressive   considerate   cooperative   efficient

intelligent   protective   solitary   wild

2 ▶ 71 Listen again and circle the best option (a, b, or c) to complete the sentences.

1 The interviewer wants to know which animals have the greatest_____ .
 a collective intelligence
 b social awareness
 c organizational skills

2 In elephant society, bull elephants_____ .
 a are dominant
 b frequently change family groups.
 c live separately

3 The story the naturalist tells concerns a young female elephant who_____ .
 a was rejected by her own family
 b couldn't find her own family
 c left the herd when she was one year old

4 What was strange was that the matriarch of the herd_____ .
 a knew who was guilty without seeing the incident
 b protected an elephant that wasn't her daughter
 c knew that the young elephant was injured

5 The purpose of the experiment in Thailand was to see if elephants_____ .
 a were different from other species
 b reacted to rewards
 c were naturally cooperative

6 The experiment_____ .
 a supports other evidence
 b does not prove elephants behave like this in the wild
 c proved how intelligent elephants are

Grammar adverbs and adverbial phrases

3 Look at the excerpts (1–4) from the interview. First, underline the adverb or adverbial phrase in each sentence. Then match them with the correct grammatical description (a–d).

1 I mean, which animals are the most socially aware? _____

2 Which species treats other members of its group in a considerate way? _____

3 They either leave voluntarily or are pushed out. _____

4 One way or another, they don't remain long in the family group. _____

a verb + adverb

b adverb + adjective

c adverb with the same form as the adjective

d adverb formed with an adverbial phrase rather than the -ly suffix

4 Look at the elephant facts. The adverbs and adverbial phrases are in the wrong place. Rewrite the sentences, putting the adverbs or adverbial phrases in the correct position. Add commas if necessary.

1 Elephants eat normally around 200 kilos of food a day.

_____

2 Although they walk faster than us (approx. seven km/h), elephants still move in a leisurely way around.

_____

3 However, they can move if they need to fast at speeds of up to forty kilometers per hour.

_____

4 Elephants do not "run" because they do not lift technically all feet off the ground at the same time.

_____

5 In spite of their thick skin, elephants are sensitive to touch extremely and can feel a fly if it lands on them.

_____

6 Male elephants leave the herd when typically they become "teenagers."

_____

7 Elephants have excellent memories, undoubtedly, which they use to remember the whereabouts of food and water.

_____

8 Around fifty elephants are killed every day for their ivory illegally.

_____

5 Look at these other sentences from the interview. Rewrite the adjective in parentheses in the correct adverbial form. Then place it in the correct place in the sentence.

1 What makes them intelligent? (social)
2 This is documented. (good)
3 She was wandering around. (disoriented)
4 This group rejected her—they pushed her away. (literal)
5 She marched over to the other herd. (straight)
6 She seemed to know which of the elephants in the other herd had been responsible. (strange)
7 If they pulled on their rope, a table with corn on it appeared before them. (simultaneous)
8 The elephants learned to coordinate their pulling. (fast)

Vocabulary social actions

6 Complete the text with these verbs.

do   have   lend   play   show   take

I think it's very important that all sections of society—young and old, rich and poor— [1]_____ a part in the life of their community. Of course, some will be able to contribute more than others, but in fact everyone can [2]_____ their part. The first thing is to [3]_____ your say in decisions that affect you. That means voting at elections or taking part in debates. If you don't do this, you can't complain when things don't go as you want them to. The second thing is to [4]_____ concern for those who are less fortunate than you: for example, to [5]_____ a helping hand to an elderly neighbor if there is something they cannot manage to do. The last thing is to be aware that the local environment is there to be enjoyed by everyone, so everyone must [6]_____ responsibility for keeping it clean and pleasant.

7 Dictation animal facts

▶ 72 Listen to five facts about animals. Complete the facts.

1 Research suggests that crows _____
_____
_____ .

2 If one dolphin _____
_____
_____ .

3 Meerkats _____ :
_____
_____ .

4 Young _____
_____
_____ .

5 Killer _____
_____
_____ .

10b How play made our world

Reading the influence of games

1 Read the article about Steven Johnson's book, *Wonderland: How Play Made the Modern World*. Find and underline two sentences that sum up his main argument in the book.

2 Write down one "serious" innovation that each of these toys or games were part of the story of, according to Johnson.

　1　Banu Musa's robotic elephant

　　　_____

　2　Vaucanson's music box　_____

　3　Pokémon Go　_____

3 Look at the article again and explain what these phrases mean in this context.

　1　It usually works the other way around (para 1)

　　　_____

　2　a golden age (para 2)

　　　_____

　3　they led to huge transformations (para 2)

　　　_____

　4　a "programmable" weaving machine (para 4)

　　　_____

　5　confined to the past (para 5)

　　　_____

How play made our world

We tend to think of play as one of the benefits of technological progress. But actually, according to Steven Johnson, author of *Wonderland: How Play Made the Modern World*, it usually works the other way around. Many of our most important innovations have their origins in human beings just having a little fun.

One of the key examples he gives is a place in Baghdad during the Islamic golden age called the House of Wisdom. Here two brothers, the Banu Musa, designed various toys like robotic elephants or automated flute players. Not only were these engineering feats ahead of their time (they appeared 400–500 years later in Western Europe), but they led to huge transformations, like industrialization and mechanization.

In the 18th century, another golden age of innovation, a Frenchman, Jacques de Vaucanson, took one of the ideas of the Banu Musa—the music box—and improved on it. He created a rotating cylinder with little pins in it that corresponded to the song you wanted to play. This is still the principle used in most music boxes today.

Little did anyone realize at the time the huge implications this invention would have, because Vaucanson did not stop there. He then began to think about how this system could be used for other purposes, such as weaving patterns in cloth. His idea, taken up by Joseph-Marie Jacquard, became a "programmable" weaving machine, the Jacquard loom, which revolutionized textile design and production. In turn, this had great influence on the ideas of Charles Babbage, who invented the first computers. And all this came from a music box, in other words, from our desire to play.

Johnson says that in no way is this phenomenon confined to the past. "We find the future wherever people are having the most fun." He points to the video game, Pokémon Go, where players run around capturing imaginary monsters in the real world. The game overlays a virtual experience on a real-world environment, a technology otherwise known as augmented reality. In practical applications, augmented reality will in the future allow us to overlay useful (and serious) information onto real-world objects.

Grammar negative adverbials and inversion

4 Find three sentences that use negative adverbials and inversion in the article. Then say:

1 what the negative adverbial is in each case.

a _____ (in para 2)

b _____ (in para 4)

c _____ (in para 5)

2 why the writer has used inversion here.

_____

3 how you would rewrite the sentences without inversion.

a _____

b _____

c _____

5 Complete these sentences using ONE word in each space.

1 Only when you see it for yourself _____ you believe it.

2 I can't ask her to do that! I _____ know her.

3 No sooner had she accepted the job _____ she realized she had made a mistake.

4 I want you to know that in no way _____ this change my opinion of you.

5 We _____ go to the movies anymore. It's too expensive.

6 _____ had I opened my mouth when he told me to stop talking.

7 Not only _____ she very successful, she's _____ very modest about it.

6 Rewrite the sentences using inversion and the adverbs or adverbial phrases in bold.

1 You shouldn't drink water from the tap under any circumstances.
under no

_____

_____

2 The Queen of England very rarely attends public functions these days. She's quite elderly now.
only

_____

_____

3 As soon as the news broke, hundreds of journalists gathered at the presidential palace to get more details.
no sooner

_____

_____

4 You can only apply for a working visa when you have been in the country for five years.
only when

_____

_____

5 I've never heard such nonsense.
never

_____

_____

6 I'd had time to put on my waterproof jacket when the most torrential rain started.
barely

_____

_____

7 Pronunciation sentence stress

a ▶ 73 Underline the two words that you think are most stressed in these sentences. Then listen and check.

1 Under no circumstances should you open it.

2 We barely speak anymore.

3 Not only did he win; he won convincingly.

4 It's hardly a success, is it?

Vocabulary having fun

8 Put the words in each expression into the right order to complete these sentences.

1 Don't keep looking up the answers on the internet. / takes / of / fun / it / out / the / it /.

_____

2 A good example of / a / making / on / words / play / is this joke: Q. Why did the actor fall through the floor? A. It was just a stage he was going through.

_____

3 I think you were very mean to / joke / on / a / play / Katja.

_____

4 Try to / see / it / of / the / funny / side /. At least you didn't break a leg.

_____

10c Rebuilding society

Listening Leymah Gbowee

1 ▶74 Listen to the story of Nobel Prize winner Leymah Gbowee and answer the questions.

1 What did she win her Nobel Prize for?

_____

2 Whose help did she enlist to achieve her aim?

_____

3 What does she do now?

_____

_____

2 ▶74 Listen again and complete these facts.

1 Liberia had suffered for many years from a _____ .

2 Gbowee became the head of a _____ movement.

3 When she returned to Liberia, she trained as a _____ .

4 She believed that in order to move forward, victims must _____ the person who wronged them.

5 She mobilized women and mothers to renew _____ in society.

6 Ultimately, their actions led to _____ .

3 ▶75 Read the excerpt about reconciliation from Gbowee's book. The words in italics are synonyms of the actual words used. Complete the excerpt with the actual words Gbowee used. Then listen and check.

> The person who *injured* [1]_____ you … If you are still angry at that person, if you haven't been able to forgive, you are *tied* [2]_____ to him. When someone *insults* [3]_____ you and you haven't let go, every time you see him, you grow breathless or your heart *misses* [4]_____ a beat. Perhaps even you *wish for* [5]_____ revenge. Above you is the Mountain of Peace and Prosperity, where we all want to go. But when you try to climb that hill, the person you haven't forgiven weighs you down. It's a personal choice whether or not to let go. But you can't *progress* [6]_____ until you break that chain.

4 Match the words from the story (1–6) with the correct synonym (a–f).

1 meaningful _____   a determined
2 tireless _____   b group
3 underpin _____   c leaflet
4 reconcile _____   d significant
5 faction _____   e be at the heart of
6 flyer _____   f bring together

Word focus *free*

5 Complete the idioms in these conversations using one or two words in each space.

1 A: Katie just went to India for a month, leaving Jack to look after the kids.

   B: Yes, I heard that. She**'s a free** _____ .

2 A: I thought they were giving their advice for free, but they sent me a bill for $300!

   B: Well, **there's no such thing as a free** _____ .

3 A: Did you attend last night's town hall meeting?

   B: I did. It started out calm and orderly but ended up being a **free-** _____ by the end.

4 A: Can I just borrow your phone for a minute to check the movie listings?

   B: Sure, _____ **free**.

5 A: Do I have to follow any particular guidelines?

   B: No, you have a **free** _____ . Do whatever you think is best.

10d Showing interest

Real life making conversation

1 ▶ 76 TED Talks are short educational talks given by experts in various fields, which are then posted on the internet. Have you ever watched one? Listen to a short conversation about a TED Talk and answer the questions.

1 What was this TED Talk about?

_____

2 What idea did the speaker in the talk criticize?

_____

_____

3 What does he suggest we do instead?

_____

_____

2 Which of these points are characteristics of a good listener? Check (✓) the three points that the person listening to the description in Exercise 1 did.

a showed appreciation ☐

b tried to predict what the other person was going to say ☐

c waited before giving their views ☐

d asked questions ☐

e related what they heard to their own experience ☐

3 Speaking skill showing interest

▶ 77 Both speakers used short responses and phrases to show interest, to agree, and to make the conversation flow more easily. Complete the phrases. Then listen and check your answers.

1 A: What are you doing?

   B: _____ a TED Talk on my laptop.

2 A: He's a really good speaker, actually.

   B: Yes, he is, _____ ?

3 B: Yeah, well, I'd go along with that.

   A: Hmm, me _____ .

4 B: I hadn't thought about it like that before.

   A: No, me _____ .

5 A: And he's saying that that can be pretty crushing for people.

   B: Yes, I _____ .

6 A: Should I send you the link?

   B: Yes, _____ .

7 B: Is it very long?

   A: I haven't gotten to the end yet, but I _____ .

4 Pronunciation elision

a ▶ 78 Which words and sounds are elided (disappear) in these short responses? Underline the sounds that you think are not pronounced. Then listen and check your answers.

1 I doubt it.

2 I expect so.

3 I'm afraid not.

4 I suppose so.

5 It's a good idea, isn't it?

b Practice saying the responses in Exercise 4a in the same way.

5 Listen and respond showing interest

▶ 79 Imagine you are with some friends. Your friends ask you some questions or make statements. Respond with your own words. Then compare what you say with the model answer that follows.

1

> What are you doing this evening?

> Staying in, I think.

10e Social mobility

Writing a discursive essay

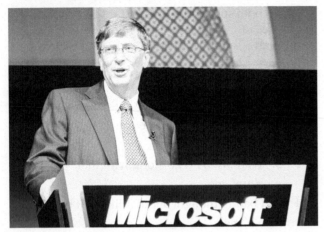

1 Despite dropping out of college, Bill Gates managed to build a hugely successful company, Microsoft. How do you think he was able to achieve this? Can you think of anyone else who has done something similar?

_____

_____

2 Look at the essay topic and think about whether you agree with it. Then read the essay and answer the questions.

"With hard work and dedication, anyone can achieve anything they want in life." Discuss.

1   What is the writer's main argument?

2   What evidence does she provide to support it?

3 Writing skill referring to evidence

a Find and underline two verbs in the second paragraph that refer to what the evidence tells us.

b Rewrite the sentences below using the verbs in bold.

1   This example shows that people with good social skills go further in life.
   illustrates
   This _____ .

2   This example implies that people with good social skills are likely to go further in life.
   infer
   We _____ .

3   This demonstrates without doubt that the workplace is changing.
   proves
   This _____ .

4   This example indicates that there is a big difference between those with good social skills and those without.
   points to
   This example _____ .

4 Write your own discursive essay on the same subject.

"With hard work and dedication, anyone can achieve anything they want in life." Discuss.

Organize your essay into three paragraphs and use as evidence a study from the University of California that showed that people who have a positive mental attitude were more successful in their careers.

In modern society, we are often told that we can achieve anything if we want it enough and are prepared to work hard enough. No goal is out of reach: successful businessperson, top medical surgeon, even president. Clearly, without hard work and dedication, you will achieve little. But is this really all there is to it? My belief is that your ability to manage relationships with others as you progress through your career is at least as important, if not a more important factor.

A recent survey conducted in Singapore suggests that it is social skills, not academic qualifications, that will have the greatest influence on success in the future. Researchers questioned various organizations, both commercial and non-commercial, to find out what skills they valued most highly in their employees. The ability to listen, to work with colleagues, and to persuade others were all at the top of their lists. This implies that human interaction, rather than analytical skills, is becoming a more important aspect of the modern workplace compared to the workplace of the past.

This does not mean that we should ignore other types of job training. However, it does mean that we should put more emphasis on the development of social and communication skills at school and university. Simply telling students that they can achieve anything they want through hard work will only lead to disappointment when they find themselves socially unprepared for the wider world.

Wordbuilding animal verbs

1 Read the example with the animal verb in bold. Then answer the questions below.

I was waiting at the traffic light when a car suddenly **rammed** into me.

1 What kind of animal is a ram? What is it known for doing?

2 What does the verb *ram* mean?

2 Look at these other animals and think about what each is known for. Then complete the sentences with the correct animal verb.

bug	duck	hound
monkey	parrot	wolf

1 He's always trying to _____ out of doing the housework.

2 Please don't _____ around. This is a serious business.

3 I wish my little brother wouldn't _____ me while I'm studying, It's very annoying.

4 Why does he always _____ down his food? It can't be good for his digestion.

5 It can't be easy being famous, especially when press photographers _____ you all the time.

6 I wish he wouldn't always just _____ the views of other people. Why doesn't he try to think for himself for once?

Learning skills speaking skills

3 Even at your level of English, you may sometimes feel frustrated at not having the right expressions for everyday situations. Try to build your range of these expressions. Look at the following situations. What would be a natural thing to say in each?

1 Someone tries to help you fix your computer, but can't. You say:

_____

2 You give someone a ride to the station. The next day, they bring you a box of chocolates. You say:

_____

3 Someone says they will be seeing a former colleague of yours tomorrow. You say:

_____

4 On a bus, someone says: "You're standing on my foot." You say:

_____

5 A colleague invites you to lunch, but you have too much work to do. You say:

_____

4 Think of other everyday situations where you are not sure what would be the right thing to say. Ask your teacher what the correct phrase would be. Keep a note of these phrases.

Check!

5 Look at the words and phrases (a–h) that describe the stories about society and communities that you learned about in Student Book Unit 10. Match two words or phrases with each photo.

a collective intelligence

b rich cultural heritage

c letting go

d colonies

e free spirits

f lose oneself in the present

g second-generation immigrants

h hunter-gatherers

_____

_____

_____
_____

_____
_____

Unit 11 Reason and emotion

11a Hikikomori

Listening a lost generation

1 ▶ 80 Listen to a radio report on people in Japan known as "hikikomori." Answer the questions.

1 Where do hikikomori spend their time?

_____

2 Who does this condition mainly affect?

_____

3 What two things could be responsible for it?

_____

2 ▶ 80 Listen again and circle the correct option (a, b, or c) to complete each statement.

1 What do people who pity the hikikomori say they are a sign of?

  a a society that is too selfish

  b a society that isn't working

  c a society that ignores its youth

2 Which of these adjectives does NOT describe how hikikomori feel?

  a angry b depressed c insecure

3 The Hikikomori condition is associated with:

  a Western society.

  b Japanese society.

  c wealthy people.

4 In the past, male university graduates in Japan could expect to get:

  a lifelong employment.

  b society's respect.

  c well-paid jobs.

5 It is suggested that the parents of hikikomori cannot accept:

  a their children's failure.

  b their children's immaturity.

  c their own poor parenting.

6 The speaker says that hikikomori need to be helped to:

  a understand their personal feelings.

  b discover their lost confidence.

  c become more sociable again.

3 Complete the expressions used by the speaker using these verbs.

inclined   locked   pulled   trod

1 … it's high time that these young people _____ **themselves together**. _____

2 But their children are _____ **in a cycle of depression** … _____

3 … middle-class Japanese males _____ **a** fairly **sure path** from high school to university … _____

4 … companies **are less** _____ **to** offer long-term employment. _____

4 Match the expressions in Exercise 3 (1–4) with their meanings (a–d).

  a don't really want to

  b followed a route

  c recovered control of their emotions

  d unable to escape from a repeating pattern

Grammar unreal past forms

5 Look at these examples of the unreal past (1–4) from the radio report. Match them with their uses (a–d).

1 It's high time that they **pulled** themselves together. _____

2 Many end up wishing they **had not worked** so hard for this empty dream. _____

3 The young hikikomori wish they **could emulate** their parents' success. _____

4 If only the parents **would act** more firmly, the critics say, the problem would not exist. _____

a describes a wish for action to do or stop doing something

b describes something not yet done that needs to be done urgently

c describes a wish about a past situation

d describes a wish about a present situation

6 Complete these sentences by putting the verbs in the correct tense. Sometimes there is more than one possibility.

1 Supposing you _____ (be) in my position, what _____ (you / do)?

2 If only we _____ (leave) earlier, we _____ (not / get) stuck in all this rush hour traffic.

3 I wish you _____ (live) nearer. Then we _____ (be) able to meet up more often.

4 It's time that we _____ (stop) treating these people as problems and _____ (realize) that they actually need our help.

5 I wish that he _____ (just / talk) to someone about what he is feeling, rather than bottling it all up inside.

Grammar extra prepositional phrases + *-ing*

7 Rewrite the sentences using prepositional phrases with *-ing*. You will need to change or add words.

E.g. If only parents would act more firmly. Instead, they shield their children from the outside world.
*If only parents would act more firmly **instead of shielding** their children from the outside world.*

1 He wrote the letter without any thought for the consequences it might have.

He wrote the letter without _____ _____ .

2 I'm not against a face-to-face meeting with them, but Skyping would be easier.

I'm not against _____ .

3 Before we decide, should we ask Naomi what she thinks about it?

Before _____ ?

4 I was able to log onto the computer with your old password.

I was able to log onto the computer by _____ .

Vocabulary feelings: adjectives and idioms

8 Match the strong feelings with the milder ones.

Strong	Mild
1 astonished ____	a content
2 ecstatic ____	b annoyed
3 livid ____	c despondent
4 miserable ____	d scared
5 petrified ____	e taken aback

9 Match the idioms (1–7) describing feelings with the adjectives (a–g).

1 all over the place ____	a optimistic
	b nervous
2 a little down ____	c confused and disorganized
3 hot under the collar ____	d astonished
4 on edge ____	e angry
5 speechless ____	f ecstatic
6 thrilled ____	g fed up
7 upbeat ____	

10 Complete the sentences using an appropriate adjective or idiom from Exercises 8 and 9. Sometimes there is more than one possibility.

1 Don't worry about Marta. She's just _____ because she has to work on a public holiday.

2 We've had a great season and are feeling very _____ about our chances of winning the league this year.

3 It was a great opportunity to get a free vacation, so I was rather _____ when he refused.

4 I'm not going out tonight. I've been working all day, and I'm _____ .

5 She's _____ that everyone else knew about the concert but that no one told her. She really wanted to go.

6 I have a good job and a nice place to live. On the whole, I'm pretty _____ .

7 I always feel _____ before I have to give a talk, but once I begin I'm fine.

8 Sorry, I can't help you. We just moved to a new house and I'm _____ at the moment.

11b Don't overthink it

Reading making hard decisions

1 Look at the question and then read the statements by four different people. Which one best describes you?

What part do reason and emotion play when you have to make a difficult decision?

In the case of difficult decisions, I always try to let fate decide—in other words, let the decision be taken out of my hands. So supposing there was a popular show I wanted to see but the tickets were really expensive. I'd wait a couple of days and then call up to buy the tickets. If they had sold out, then I'd accept that and go 'Oh, well, maybe it wasn't for me, anyway.' But if there were still some left, then I'd buy them. In either case, I would feel that fate had decided for me. AB

When it comes to difficult decisions, I often find I just have to go with my gut feeling. If I try to use reason, sometimes I go around and around in circles because there are just too many factors to consider. I think what's important is not to have regrets once you've made a decision. So if you've made the choice to move to a new apartment, don't start torturing yourself with thoughts like, 'If I'd stayed where I was, I'd probably have been much happier.' JT

You're going to think this idea is a bit forced, but I find the easiest way to make a difficult decision is to use a points system. So, for example, if you're thinking about whether to take a new job or not, then make a list of advantages and disadvantages. Put a score of one or two points next to each advantage and a score of minus one or two next to each disadvantage. Then add them up and see if the total is positive or negative. PT

People say that you shouldn't let your feelings interfere with your decisions. But anyone who says they can make decisions in a completely rational way is kidding themselves. You can't just shut off your feelings. At some point, you'll have to deal with them. So I think you just need to accept that and accept that making the wrong decision now and then is just part of life. CL

2 Read the statements again and check (✓)which speaker(s):

1 stress(es) a logical approach to decision-making.
   ☐ AB   ☐ JT   ☐ PT   ☐ CL

2 think(s) that you should listen to your emotions when making a decision.
   ☐ AB   ☐ JT   ☐ PT   ☐ CL

3 don't/doesn't really have any particular method for decision-making.
   ☐ AB   ☐ JT   ☐ PT   ☐ CL

4 stress(es) the importance of not looking back at decisions once they have been made.
   ☐ AB   ☐ JT   ☐ PT   ☐ CL

5 is/are resigned to the fact that they will not get every decision right.
   ☐ AB   ☐ JT   ☐ PT   ☐ CL

6 try/tries to detach themselves from the decision-making process.
   ☐ AB   ☐ JT   ☐ PT   ☐ CL

3 Underline the phrases in the statements that mean the following:

1 allow something to stop being in my control (AB)
2 instinct (JT)
3 not make any progress (JT)
4 making yourself suffer (JT)
5 unnatural (PT)
6 is deceiving themselves (CL)

Grammar conditionals and inversion

4 Rewrite these conditional sentences from the text as inverted conditional forms using the prompts.

1 If there were still some left, I'd buy them.
Were _____ .

2 If I'd stayed where I was, I'd probably have been much happier.
Had _____ .

3 If you're thinking about whether to take a new job or not, then make a list of advantages and disadvantages.
Should _____ .

5 Complete these conditional sentences by putting the verb in the correct form.

1 I think if I _____ (take) the job, it will probably lead to other opportunities.

2 If I _____ (not / leave) when I did, I think I _____ (still / be) there now.

3 Life _____ (be) easier if people _____ (spend) more time on simple decisions and less time on complicated ones.

4 If you _____ (doubt) what I say, read Jonah Lehrer's book *How We Decide*.

5 If my husband _____ (not / have) a well-paid job in London, we _____ (move) to the countryside years ago.

6 Things would be very different if I _____ (know) then what I know now.

6 Rewrite sentences 1–6 from Exercise 5 as inverted conditionals using the words in parentheses.

1 _____
_____ (Were … to)

2 _____
_____ (Had)

3 _____
_____ (were …. to)

4 _____
_____ (Should)

5 _____
_____ (if not for)

6 _____
_____ (had)

7 Pronunciation heteronyms

a ▶ 81 Look at the sentences and decide how *-ate* is pronounced (/ət/ or /eɪt/) in each word in bold. Then listen and check your answers.

1 They sent us four **duplicate** copies of the contract to sign.
2 Can you just **elaborate** on that?
3 I wish I were as **articulate** as Beth.
4 They had to **deliberate** for a long time before coming to a decision.
5 Please **separate** the recyclable waste from the nonrecyclable.

b ▶ 82 Listen to these heteronyms and underline the stress in each word in bold. What rule can you make about these words?

1 a What's that strange **object**?
   b I don't **object** to the idea.
2 a Did they **contest** the decision?
   b It wasn't a fair **contest**.
3 a How much did the price **increase**?
   b It's a big **increase**.
4 a What an interesting **project**.
   b We can't **project** far into the future.
5 a We **import** furniture from Japan.
   b Our main **import** is sugar.

8 Dictation a personal decision

▶ 83 Listen to someone describing a decision they had to make. Complete the paragraph. Then say what you think they should do.

OK, so here's _____

_____

_____

_____

_____

_____

_____

_____

_____

_____

11c RoboBees

Listening **insect robots**

1 ▶ 84 Look at the photo and the title *Insect robots*. Answer the questions. Then listen to a report about RoboBees and check your answers.

1 What technical challenges do you think a designer of an insect robot faces?

_____

2 What useful tasks could insect robots perform?

_____

> **hive** (n) /haɪv/ a house for bees to live in
> **pollinate** (v) /ˈpɒləneɪt/ to take pollen from one flower to another so that it can produce seeds

2 ▶ 85 Answer the questions. Then listen to the first part of the report again and check your answers.

1 What inspired the scientists to make RoboBee?

_____

2 What did they think they could use RoboBee to do?

_____

3 What do they hope to create with RoboBee?

_____

4 What will RoboBee use to respond to its environment?

_____

3 ▶ 86 The speaker made a number of comparisons between RoboBee and real bees. Listen to the second part of the report again and complete the chart.

	RoboBee	Actual bees
1	uses a computer chip brain	have a _____
2	_____	are amazing flying machines
3	uses a hive as a _____	live in a real bee hive
4	has a variety of purposes	make _____ and _____
5	uses cameras and sensors to navigate	use _____

4 ▶ 87 Listen to the last part of the report again and complete the summary. Use one or two words per blank.

Bees are not the only animals to have
¹ _____ roboticists. Scientists have also used flies, fish, and ² _____ to get ideas for robots. It is hoped that such research will create a new generation of machines based on the designs of ³ _____ , using the ⁴ _____ that animals apply in the task of daily survival. The National ⁵ _____ Foundation in the United States is convinced of the potential benefits and is putting ⁶ _____ per year into the research.

5 Complete these collocations from the report with the correct verb.

> adapt to   determine   face
> flap   perform   take

1 _____ an operation
2 _____ changing conditions
3 _____ a challenge
4 _____ one's wings
5 _____ the cause of something
6 _____ advantage of

Word focus *beyond*

6 Underline the correct word to complete these expressions with *beyond*.

1 I last saw her when she was fifteen, so she had changed **beyond all** *appreciation / recognition*.

2 It's **beyond** *me / my thinking* how anyone can be so talented and so lazy at the same time.

3 Her loyalty to the company is **beyond** *doubt / uncertainty*.

4 Risking his life to save others from the fire was **beyond the call of** *service / duty*.

5 My father was an extravagant man who always **lived beyond his** *income / means*.

11d You look concerned

Real life recognizing feelings

1 ▶ 88 Listen to three workplace conversations. Write the number of the conversation that discusses each subject. There are two extra subjects.

_____ a someone worried that others have the wrong impression of them

_____ b someone upset that they were not asked to a meeting

_____ c what one person thought about another's proposals

_____ d someone saying something too directly

_____ e a joke that was taken the wrong way

2 ▶ 88 Listen again and answer the questions.

1 In Conversation 1, why is the second speaker upset with the first speaker?
_____

2 In Conversation 2, what does the second speaker worry that Sarah might think about her now?
_____

3 In Conversation 3, is Gary likely to be offended by what the second speaker said?
_____

3 ▶ 88 The speakers used phrases to acknowledge the emotional effect of what they said. Complete the phrases. Use one word per blank. Then listen and check your answers.

Conversation 1

1 You _____ a _____ taken aback. I didn't mean to _____ you during the meeting.

2 Anyway, I'm sorry if that _____ _____ wrong at the meeting.

Conversation 2

3 You _____ worried. Is something bothering you?

4 Did I _____ something to _____ you?

Conversation 3

5 Sorry, why are you laughing? I don't understand what's _____ _____ .

6 Sorry, maybe that _____ a little abrupt.

4 Pronunciation adjectives ending in -ed

a ▶ 89 Are the following -ed endings pronounced /d/, /t/, or /ɪd/? Listen and check your answers.

1 shocked _____   6 minded _____
2 thrilled _____   7 surprised _____
3 worried _____   8 impressed _____
4 bored _____   9 frustrated _____
5 frightened _____   10 laughed _____

b Practice saying the words in Exercise 4a in the same way.

c ▶ 90 Listen to these words. What sound does -ied produce here?

1 terrified   3 mystified
2 preoccupied   4 satisfied

5 Listen and respond being sensitive

▶ 91 Imagine you are having discussions with colleagues at work. You want to understand the feelings behind what they are saying. Listen to each statement. Respond with your own words. Then compare your response with the model answer that follows.

1
> *Well, I'm a little surprised that you volunteered me for the project.*

> *Oh, I'm sorry. I hope I didn't upset you. I didn't mean to put you in a difficult situation.*

11e Don't get me wrong

Writing an email message

1 Writing skill avoiding misunderstandings

Read emails 1–4 and underline the phrases that help the reader avoid a misunderstanding.

1 Hi John,

I'm still waiting to hear back from you about buying some of my old furniture. Were you that horrified when you saw it? I'm joking, of course! I don't want to pressure you in any way—it's just that I'm moving in two weeks and I need to know what I'm doing.

Let me know.

Best wishes,

Hakim

2 Dear Megan,

Many thanks for getting back to me so quickly. In your haste, you attached the wrong document. It's the photo of the main university entrance that I need, not the one of your vacation in Mexico! Can you resend?

Thanks.

Jen

3 Dear Sarah,

Just to let you know that we won't need you on Sunday after all. Frederica has volunteered to help us with the packing. Please don't take this the wrong way. We do really appreciate your offer.

See you soon, I hope.

Paul

4 Hi Barney,

That wasn't the answer I expected! I thought you wanted to be involved in this project. Don't worry—I'm not offended in any way. It just took me slightly by surprise.

Speak soon.

Mike

2 Read emails 5–8 and match them with the impression that they give (a–d).

a This person seems offended not to be asked. _____

b This person seems too busy to deal with correspondence. _____

c This person seems annoyed to be kept waiting. _____

d This person seems to be making a rude comment about the reader. _____

5 Hi Dean,

That was a very long answer you sent me. I will reply to you when I have time to read it properly.

Jeff

6 Dear Brigitte,

Great to hear from you! Your spelling hasn't improved much since we were in school. I had to reread your email three times before I could understand it. Your idea of meeting up on December 8th sounds perfect. Let me know where.

All the best,

Rosalie

7 Dear Mr. Nasri,

I sent you a quotation as promised a week ago, but you have not replied. Are we to suppose that you are not interested?

Kind regards,

David Temperley

8 Dear Ben,

I received your email saying that you don't want to take me up on my offer of advice about the design of your website. I hope the person you have found to help you with this does a good job.

Yours,

Jasper

3 Rewrite emails 5–8 so that you avoid the possibility of the reader misunderstanding or being offended by them.

Wordbuilding heteronyms

1 Match the words (1–7) with their definitions (a–g).

  1 delegate (n) /'delɪgət/ _____
  2 alternate (v) /'ɔːltərneɪt/ _____
  3 wound (n) /wuːnd/ _____
  4 tear (n) /tɪr/ _____
  5 minute (n) /'mɪnɪt/ _____
  6 sewer (n) /'səʊr/ _____
  7 refuse (v) /rɪ'fjuːz/ _____

  a someone who works with a needle and thread
  b change places periodically
  c say no to something
  d a drop of water from the eye
  e a unit of time
  f a representative
  g a cut or injury

2 Look at the words in bold. What part of speech are they? What do they mean? How are they pronounced?

  1 I **wound** a piece of bandage around the cut to protect it from infection.

    _____

  2 Please try not to **tear** the material when you put the cover back on the chair. It's very tight.

    _____

  3 I put a **minute** amount of sugar in your coffee before I remembered you didn't take sugar. You won't taste it.

    _____

  4 We share a single job. We work on **alternate** days of the week.

    _____

  5 It is well known that rats live in the **sewers**.

    _____

  6 Household **refuse** collection is on Thursdays.

    _____

  7 Good managers learn how to **delegate** responsibility to their team.

    _____

Learning skills the internet

3 The internet has some great resources for learning English. Here are a few tips for using these.

News: Visit an English-language news website and listen to a story that you are already familiar with. Write down new words that you learn.

Songs: Find a song sung in English that you like and try to write down the lyrics. Then do an internet search for the lyrics and compare.

Talks: Listen to TED Talks. These are free and are categorized by subject. Listen without the transcript and see how much you can understand. Then listen again, this time following the transcript. Make a note of any new words.

Blogs: Try to find blogs about stories that have interested you in *Life*. Perhaps post a comment on a blog and start a conversation.

4 Do one of the things in Exercise 3 this week. Then tell a fellow student about your experience.

Check!

5 Do the crossword. All the answers are in Student Book Unit 11.

Across

  1 Unit 11a was about this kind of intelligence.
  5 "You _____ worried. Is everything OK?"
  6 a little down _____
  8 the opposite of reasoned and logical

Down

  2 small facial gestures are called _____ - expressions
  3 and 7 a stronger way of saying "I wish …"
  4 the prize that Kahneman won
  5 very angry
  7 see 3 Down
  9 artificial intelligence

Unit 12 Mother nature

12a Aerial view

Listening interview with Marie Arana

1 ▶92 You are going to listen to an interview with Marie Arana, a journalist. Which kind of landscapes does she associate with North America and which with South America? Which photo(s) match(es) her descriptions of North America and which South America?

_____

_____

2 ▶92 Complete Marie Arana's descriptions of each of the places depicted in the photos. Listen again and check.

1 great _____ of grass

2 _____-_____ mountain

3 _____ , green _____

4 _____ towns

shantytown (n) /'ʃænti,taʊn/ a poor area of a town made up of shacks or insubstantial buildings
hacienda (n) /,hæsi'endə/ (of Spanish origin) a large estate used for farming
prairie (n) /'preəri/ a large area of flat grassland

3 ▶92 Listen again and circle the best option (a, b, or c).

1 Marie Arana has always had a strong awareness of landscapes because she grew up _____ .
  a near volcanoes
  b on a farm near the sea
  c on an island in the Pacific

2 The North American landscape felt foreign to her because _____ .
  a the land stretched so far in all directions
  b there were roads everywhere
  c people had settled everywhere

3 What she loves about Peru is _____ .
  a how deserted it is
  b how varied the landscape is
  c how easy it is to get from one place to another

4 Why had the cities she saw from the air grown so much?
  a because of economic migrants
  b because of people escaping various disasters
  c because of industrialization

5 How did she feel when she saw the cities of South America from the air?
  a moved and impressed
  b confused
  c surprised and saddened

6 What was the most difficult thing about taking photos from a small airplane?
  a the wind and cold coming through the open door
  b you don't have confidence in the plane
  c your equipment doesn't always work properly

4 Look at these bold words and expressions from the interview and circle the correct definition (a or b).

1 **In all truth**, I was taken aback...
   a to be honest   b in every sense

2 The urban centers have **burgeoned**...
   a grown much larger   b become depressed

3 ...the shantytowns that had **sprouted up**...
   a grown upward   b appeared and grown rapidly

4 ...the **prevailing** beauty of the land...
   a dominant   b hidden

5 ...the **visual feast** below us...
   a delight for the eyes   b confusing image

6 ...**fierce gales** rushing through the open door...
   a extreme cold   b very strong winds

Grammar approximation and vague language

5 ▶ 92 Use these expressions to add to (or replace) the words and phrases in bold. Then listen again and check.

| around | hundreds of | -ish |
| kind of | or so | over |

1 My earliest memories are of earthquakes—there were **fifteen** by the time I reached the age of five.
_____

2 ... a place where you could drive for **miles** and human beings always be in evidence.
_____

3 Having grown up in **a desert**, I had never seen great fields of grass.
_____

4 Peru has five kinds of landforms ... all of it in **close** proximity!
_____

5 ... the shantytowns that had sprouted up around the cities in the past **thirty years**.
_____

6 The sights from **1,500 meters** in the air were astoundingly beautiful!
_____

6 Add to or replace the expressions of approximation in the correct place.

> We live on a big ranch in Montana. It's been in the family for 120 years. I guess my father is what you would call a cowboy. He has a herd of 300 cattle which is actually small for this region, but it keeps us busy! I still help out there, but next year I'm going back to college to continue my studies. I think we all have ambition to do something different from our parents—I'd like to be a car designer. I have ideas. If it doesn't work out, I can always come back and help out with work on the farm.

1 odd
2 roughly
3 kind of
4 in the ... or two
5 some
6 dozens of
7 stuff

Vocabulary nature

7 Circle the best option to form collocations about descriptions of nature.

1 *dramatic / wooded / bleak* hillsides
2 *lush / sparse / cloudless* sky
3 *rugged / monotonous / rich* farmland
4 *bleak / lush / rugged* valleys
5 *snow-capped / lush / dramatic* scenery
6 *dramatic / sparse / monotonous* vegetation
7 *rugged / cloudless / sparse* terrain
8 *monotonous / rich / snow-capped* mountains

8 **Dictation approximate answers**

▶ 93 Listen to a conversation where a speaker gives approximate answers to questions. Complete the answers.

1 Where do you live now?
   _____ Irbid,
   _____.

2 Is that near where you work?
   _____
   _____.

3 What's the countryside like around there?
   _____
   _____.

4 Are you near the desert?
   _____
   _____.

12b Nature's great events

Reading nature blog

1 Have you seen any of the following events in nature? What amazing natural events would you like to see?

> a double rainbow   a solar eclipse
> a lunar eclipse

2 Read the blog about four amazing events seen by the writer. Which one(s) (AB, RT, SS, IC):

1 are a bit frightening? _____
2 have to do with the sun? _____
3 have to do with water? _____
4 are unexplained phenomena? _____

5 take place in places with cold climates? _____

6 produce an amazing effect? _____

3 Find words in the blog with the following meanings:

1 drops of water that appear on plants and the grass in cold weather (para 1) _____
2 the northernmost and southernmost points on Earth (para 2) _____
3 poisonous (para 3) _____
4 burned or made very dry by heat (para 4) _____
5 turning around and around (para 5) _____

Nature's great events

Nature can conjure up some pretty amazing spectacles. Some are on a modest scale and are easily found: a spider's web in the morning dew one autumn morning, or frost formations on a window pane. Others are on a much grander scale and are not so easy to come by. I have been lucky enough to see four such spectacles on my travels, and it's these I'd like to share with you.

The Aurora Borealis

This is an extraordinary light show in the far northern skies that I promised myself I would see one day—and I wasn't disappointed. The Aurora occurs when solar winds (a stream of plasma) interact with Earth's magnetic fields, which are strongest at the two poles. As particles in the solar wind collide with gases in the atmosphere, they glow in wonderful greens, blues, and reds.

Red tides

Also called the algal bloom, red tides are caused by an accumulation of algae in the ocean. It's an impressive, but also slightly alarming sight as the sea turns a blood-red color. The algae is not dangerous to humans (although it is toxic for animals), but it can be irritating. We would always check for news of red tides before planning beach visits.

Sailing stones

One of the strangest things I've come across is the sailing stones of Death Valley in California. These single stones sit in the middle of vast expanses of scorched open desert and—extraordinarily—they move. Stones weighing over 100 kilos drift across the sand. You would think this could be explained by the action of the wind or elements, until you learn that some stones that started in the same place have been known to move in completely different directions.

Ice circles

These are beautiful circular discs of ice, some measuring up to 150 meters across, that form in rivers. Most of us are used to seeing ice forming at the edge of rivers, but in the case of ice circles, it forms in the middle. They occur when a current turns slowly in a circular motion and the spinning water freezes. Ideally, I would have liked to have seen one of the larger ones, but even a twenty-meter diameter one is an amazing sight.

Grammar *would*

4 Look at the list of the uses of the modal verb *would* (1–7). Then match the sentences from the blog (a–d) with the correct use.

1 to make a polite request
2 to describe a hypothetical situation
3 to respond to a request or invitation
4 to describe a reported intention, expectation, or decision
5 to describe a habitual action in the past
6 to indicate a person or thing's refusal to do something
7 to express an opinion or a hope in a less forceful way

a This is an extraordinary light show that I promised myself I **would see** one day. _____

b We **would** always **check** for news of red tides before planning beach visits. _____

c You **would think** this could be explained by the action of the wind or elements. _____

d Ideally, I **would have liked** to have seen one of the larger ones, but .... _____

5 Read the exchanges. Rewrite the underlined sections using phrases with *would*.

A: ¹Can I ask you to do me a favor?

B: Sure. What is it?

A: ²Take this cake out of the oven in ten minutes. I have to go to the mall.

C: Do you want to come over for dinner on Saturday? We're having a few friends around.

D: That ³sounds really nice. Can I bring anything?

E: What happened? I thought you were going to drive to work this morning.

F: I was, but ⁴I couldn't get the car to start.

G: Is this where you used to live?

H: Yes, that's my old house over there. And that's the café that we ⁵used to go to most evenings.

I: Did you stop for milk on the way home?

J: No, I ⁶meant to get some, but I didn't have enough time.

K: How was Spain? Pretty hot, I ⁷expect.

L: We didn't go in the end. We decided ⁸to stay at home instead.

6 Pronunciation *would*

a ▶ 94 Look at the sentences with *would*. Listen to how the underlined words are pronounced.

1 Would you like to go for a walk?
2 I would love to come with you, but I can't.
3 I tried to talk to him, but he wouldn't listen.
4 When I was a student, I would always walk wherever I went.
5 You would imagine that she knows what she's doing.

b ▶ 94 Listen again to the sentences. Try to say each one before you hear it. Pause as necessary.

Idioms adjective collocations

7 Complete the adjective collocations with these words.

brand	fast	freezing	lightning	pitch
rock	soaking	stiff	sick	wide

1 I can't wear my coat—it's still _____ wet after I biked home in the rain.

2 Is that a _____ new computer you have?

3 I fell _____ asleep in the lecture.

4 This bread is _____ hard. Can you get some more when you're out?

5 The room was _____ black. You couldn't see your hand in front of your face.

6 What a _____ cold wind. I should have brought my hat.

7 She has _____ quick reactions. She'd make a fantastic tennis player.

8 Where have you been? I've been worried _____ about you.

9 The race is _____ open. Anyone could win.

10 I was scared _____ that he was going to fire me, but he was actually really nice.

8 Look at these other adjective collocations (1–6) and answer the questions (a and b).

1 squeaky clean   4 bored stiff
2 dirt cheap   5 filthy rich
3 silky smooth   6 razor sharp

a In which collocation does the intensifying word come second? _____

b Which make a negative judgment about the quality?

_____

12c Tigers as neighbors

Listening a lesson in conservation

1 ▶ 95 Listen to someone discussing the future survival of tigers. How does he think the tiger population, and that of other wild animals, can best be conserved?

_____

_____

2 ▶ 95 Listen again and circle the best option (a, b, or c) to complete each statement.

1 The speaker says he will feel devastated if _____ .
   a tigers become extinct
   b there are no more tigers in the wild
   c people are unable to live near tigers

2 The speaker says that personally _____ .
   a he would be happy to live near tigers
   b he admires people who live near tigers
   c he doesn't want to live near tigers

3 Before 2016, the tiger population _____ .
   a had been falling steadily
   b had risen slightly
   c had remained stable

4 Because the tribes are vegetarian _____ .
   a they don't eat tiger meat
   b they look for different food from the tigers
   c they don't look for food in dangerous places

5 Tigers are good for farmers who _____ .
   a grow crops
   b keep small animals
   c are worried about thieves

6 For the Soliga tribe, the tiger is a(n) _____ .
   a vulnerable creature
   b sacred creature
   c evil creature

7 The speaker says that local people killing tigers for their skins _____ .
   a is a real problem
   b is a concern of some
   c is very unlikely to happen

8 The speaker thinks that local tribes make good conservationists because they _____ .
   a respect other living things around them
   b understand environmental problems
   c have sophisticated land management skills

3 Complete the summary below. You have been given the first two letters of the missing words.

[1] Mu_____ as I love tigers, I don't really want to live next to one. Luckily for tiger conservation, there are people who do. The local tribes of the Western Ghats of India [2] co_____ happily with tigers because, as vegetarians, the people don't [3] co_____ with them for food. The result of this [4] he_____ relationship is that tiger numbers are [5] gr_____ . But conservationists think that it would be better if there were no people in these areas, so now the local tribes are being [6] ev_____ . This is [7] ir_____ because these are the very people who have made tiger conservation a success and the best chance that the tigers have of [8] su_____ .

Word focus *move*

4 Circle the correct prepositions to complete the sentences.

1 I think we should **move** *on* / *off* because this discussion is getting us nowhere.

2 Come on—**get a move** *in* / *on*. You may not want to get there on time, but I do.

3 She couldn't afford the rent on her apartment anymore, so she gave it up and **moved back** *in* / *around* with her parents.

4 If we **move** the tables and chairs *around* / *off*, we can create more space at the front of the room.

5 Her speech **moved** everyone in the room *to* / *with* **tears**.

6 Jack is one of the last original residents of this street. The rest have all **moved** *over* / *out*.

12d Environmental vandalism?

Real life a debate

1 Speaking skill interrupting

a Look at the phrases for interrupting and preventing interruptions. Complete phrases 2–8 using ONE word in each blank.

1 Yes, but …

2 Sorry, can I _____ interrupt you there?

3 Can I just _____ what I was saying?

4 No, sorry. I have to stop you _____ …

5 Can I just say something _____ answer to that?

6 No, hang _____ a minute.

7 Just a _____ , please.

8 You can _____ your point in a moment.

b Which phrases in Exercise 1a (1–8) are used to:

interrupt someone? _____

prevent interruptions? _____

2 ▶ 96 Listen to a debate between three friends about the building of a new golf course in a coastal area. Answer the questions.

a What arguments are used in favor of the new golf course?

_____

_____

b What arguments are used against the golf course?

_____

_____

3 ▶ 96 Listen again. Which phrases in Exercise 1 do the different speakers use to interrupt and to prevent interruptions?

_____

4 Pronunciation intonation in interruptions

a ▶ 97 Look at these phrases for interrupting. Listen and circle the ones that are said with a polite and firm intonation. Which one is not?

1 I have to stop you there.

2 OK, you can make your point in a moment.

3 Can I just finish what I was saying?

4 Can I just say something in answer to that?

5 Just a moment, please.

b ▶ 98 Listen again to the exception, this time said with a polite intonation. Then practice saying all the sentences in Exercise 4a.

5 Listen and respond environmental vandalism?

▶ 99 You are going to hear a debate about the building of a new golf course on an area of natural beauty in your country. You believe it is a bad idea. Listen to each statement. Respond with your own words. Then compare your response with the model answer that follows.

1

I was very pleased to hear about the new golf course. Were you?

No, I wasn't, actually. I don't see why they have to build it in a national park.

12e To the editor

Writing a letter to a newspaper

1 Read the letter and answer the questions.

1 What was the subject of the article that prompted this letter?

_____

2 What issue did the writer of the article ignore, according to the letter writer?

_____

3 What recommendations does she make to remedy this situation?

_____

2 Writing skill persuasive language

a Find examples of the following persuasive elements in the letter and underline them.

1 a personal connection with the topic (para 2)
2 a strong statement or statistic (para 2)
3 an emotive expression or phrase (para 2)
4 a short, clear sentence (para 3)
5 an appeal to shared experiences (para 4)
6 a view of what the future could be like (para 4)

b Look at these pairs of sentences and say which is more persuasive and why.

1
a With a little more thought, drivers could reduce animal injuries on the roads.
b Animal injuries are a direct result of drivers' thoughtlessness.

2
a There are huge numbers of animal deaths on the roads each year.
b A million animals are killed on the roads each day in the United States.

3
a Our careless attitude is a poor reflection on us as a species.
b By not caring about the lives of other animals, we show that we are not a very good species to live with.

4
a Such accidents are inexcusable.
b Such accidents are a shame.

To the Editor:
I enjoyed your article "Something to cheer about at last" (Tuesday June 7th), and I agree that we should be proud (of ourselves and animals) that wildlife is thriving in our cities. But there is one area where we still have a lot of progress to make with animal welfare: our roads.

I am a vet, and injury from road accidents is the most common reason animals are brought to our clinic. I am the first to accept that accidents can and do happen. What I cannot accept, however, is that we just shrug our shoulders and do nothing about it. Many accidents could be avoided if drivers were more attentive to animals on the roads. But more importantly, many animal injuries could be treated if drivers responded more sensitively to accidents.

So, be animal aware. And if you hit a wild animal while driving, stop the car safely and go and check on the animal. If it is injured, try to pick it up, protecting yourself with a thick item of clothing. Then take it to the nearest veterinary clinic. Even if the animal ultimately dies, it will have a far more humane death in the clinic than by the roadside.

We all know how upsetting it is to hit an animal in your car. But taking steps to lessen any negative consequences will make you—and the animal—feel a whole lot better.

3 Imagine you have read a newspaper article that urges drivers to be more attentive and careful when driving, especially at night, so as to avoid hitting and killing animals on the roads. Write a letter to the editor agreeing with the article. Use persuasive techniques from Exercise 2 and add the following ideas for improving the situation:
- lower speed limits on roads
- signs warning drivers that animals (deer, dogs, cats, etc.) are crossing
- laws making it illegal to drive away after hitting an animal

Wordbuilding adverb + adjective collocations

1 Look at these adverbs. Choose the most appropriate adverb to complete each sentence.

culturally	emotionally	visually
ethnically	internationally	socially
environmentally		

1 It wasn't a great story, but the effects in the movie were _____ stunning.

2 She's very natural with people and always puts them at their ease. I wish I were as _____ gifted as she is.

3 It's important to be _____ sensitive so that you don't offend other people when talking about their customs and habits.

4 He's an _____ famous composer. In fact, I think he's better known abroad than in his own country.

5 It was an _____ charged atmosphere at the meeting: a lot of people were very angry.

6 All their products are sold in _____ friendly packaging.

7 It's the most _____ diverse university in the country with over 67 different nationalities.

Learning skills eliminating errors

2 You probably now understand most of what you hear and read and are easily understood by others. But you may feel there are some gaps in your knowledge and you are not always sure you are speaking accurately. Try to follow these "social strategies" to overcome this.

1 Ask questions about the language, especially idioms or culturally specific items, when you are in the company of native speakers.

2 Check the precise meaning of words if you are not sure you are using them correctly.

3 Ask people to correct you if you make a mistake.

4 You may have some ingrained errors—mistakes that you have "grown up" with. Make an effort to eliminate these. Ask friends or native speakers if they have noticed such mistakes.

3 Look at this list of the most common types of advanced learner errors. Do you recognize any of them? Ask your teacher to give you a list of what he/she thinks are your ingrained errors.

1 mistakes with agreement (e.g., singular noun–plural verb)

2 mistakes with prepositions

3 mistakes with the present perfect tense

4 mistakes with tense choice in general

5 incorrect formation of a particular idiom or everyday expression

6 mistakes with verb patterns: gerund or infinitive or base form

4 Look at these sentences. Identify and correct the mistake in each one.

1 We must ask if it is really worth to spend all this money on something that will bring only a small benefit.

2 At the end, it is a question of personal choice for each individual.

3 I had many strange experiences in my life, but nothing compares to that.

4 The resort, like the other resorts around it, are made up of a mixture of new and old hotels.

Check!

5 Complete the items below. Then take the first letter of the answers to make the name of a part of Mother Nature. All the answers are in Student Book Unit 12.

1 _____ , hilly terrain

2 What kind of pollution prompted the letter in Unit 12e? _____ pollution

3 Where is there an extraordinary puffin population? _____

4 Moving from place to place, without a fixed home _____

5 What was the name of the Japanese poet that you read about in Unit 12b? _____

6 Complete with a preposition. "It's been six months since George split up with his girlfriend, but he still thinks about her all the time. He really needs to move _____ ."

7 Complete the adjective collocation. "Where have you been? I've been _____ sick about you."

A part of Mother Nature: _____

Audioscripts

Unit 1

▶ 01

Hello, everyone. My name's Herb Sokolowski, and I'm a college graduate, just like you. You might have heard of me, because I used to have a TV program called *Weird Science*. Currently, I'm writing a book about scientific inventions, and when I was asked to come and speak to you, I thought I'd talk about that. But then I thought: "What's the use of that? It'll probably only interest a few of them." So instead, I'm going to give you some rules of life that I read about 15 years ago in a book by a guy called Charles Sykes. I believe the book was called *Dumbing Down Our Kids*. Before that, I had believed myself to be—as you probably do now—one entitled individual. But it changed my attitude and, who knows, perhaps it'll change yours. I've reduced the number of rules a little and put them in my own words. So, are you ready? Here we go.

RULE 1: Life's not fair; get used to it.

RULE 2: You will not make eighty thousand dollars next year. You won't be a vice president, not until you've earned the right.

RULE 3: If you think your teacher is tough, wait till you get a boss.

RULE 4: Flipping burgers is not beneath your dignity. Many years ago, your grandparents had a different word for burger flipping; they called it opportunity.

RULE 5: If you mess up, it's probably your own fault. So don't whine about your mistakes: learn from them.

RULE 6: You probably thought growing up that your parents were pretty boring. But they were like that because at the time they were paying your bills, washing your clothes, and listening to you talk about how cool you are. So before you go off and save the world, clean up your own room.

RULE 7: Over the last twenty years, schools have abolished the idea of winners and losers—but life hasn't. In school, they give you as much time as you want to get the right answer. That rarely happens in real life.

RULE 8: Be nice to nerds. Sooner or later, you'll end up working for one.

▶ 02

One of the problems with advice is that people tend to interpret it to suit their own purposes. An example of this is the wisdom of the 18th-century economist Adam Smith. One of his main ideas was that if you allow people to seek wealth for themselves, they will naturally create jobs and wealth for others. He called this "the invisible hand." People trying to improve their own situation also help their neighbor improve theirs, but without meaning to, as if with an invisible hand. Unfortunately, a lot of people took Smith to mean that it was all right to be greedy and selfish and not to help others directly, which is not at all what he meant.

▶ 04

Like many islands, Great Britain and its language, English, have been subject to many influences over the centuries. What developed as a result is a language with a very rich and large vocabulary. Later in British history, the influenced would become an influencer, an exporter of its language and culture, to a point where its language again became subject to changes made by others who use it to communicate with each other in the worlds of business or academia.

The first influence is that of the Romans and their language, Latin. The legacy of the Romans is evident in the Latin-based or Romance languages that still survive in many Western European countries. However, after the fall of the Roman Empire in the fifth century, Britain was invaded by various Germanic peoples and it was their languages, notably Anglo-Saxon, or what is now known as Old English, that became the dominant force.

When William I of Normandy conquered Britain in 1066, he established French as the official language, but instead of replacing English, French was assimilated into it, and Middle English, a close relation to the language, is still spoken in Britain today. This is a language made up of German vocabulary and simplified German grammar mixed with French-derived—often Latin-based—words. The language continued to remain rather organic until the invention of the printing press and the wider publication of the written word, when it started to become standardized. You can see this very clearly if you compare the writing of the poet Chaucer in the 14th century, which is difficult to understand without reference to a glossary, with Shakespeare's writing two centuries later. Shakespeare is not easy, but in fact it is relatively similar to the English of today.

From this point in history—the 17th century through to the end of the 19th century—British colonialism thrived. This had two implications for the English language: the first was the importation into the language of yet more words—*pajama* and *bungalow*, for example, from India; the second was the spread of English around the globe—to India, America, East Africa, and so on. With its spread came adaptation. Each country stamped its own mark on the language used, making it something different from the English spoken in Britain. The writer George Bernard Shaw famously spoke of Britain and the United States as "two nations divided by a common language." The new English-speaking settlers in America wanted to set their language and their country apart from Britain, and so brought in new words and new spellings, as well as a new, more direct style of speaking.

People have argued that English was successful in its global reach because it was a versatile and flexible language. But in fact its spread had far more to do with economic factors. People needed a language to do business in, and English was in the right place at the right time.

Which brings us to the present day and to a situation where many versions of English now exist. The writer Robert McCrum has identified two types in particular: English as spoken by native speakers in different countries around the world and Globish, a simplified form of the language used by non-native speakers to communicate on matters of business or work. According to McCrum, this is a utilitarian kind of English where you learn a limited vocabulary—maybe 1,500 words at most—and grammar, enough to enable you to do your job at the call center, for example.

Although this characterization is too simplistic—there are many shades and versions of English between Globish and the language of Shakespeare—it does make an important point: that English, like any language, is a tool that people adapt and exploit to suit their needs. No one version is right or wrong; the question, rather, is which version you aspire to speak.

▶ 05

Conversation 1
T: What did you think of the talk?
A: Yeah, I thought it was really interesting: a lot of food for thought.
T: Sorry, I should have introduced myself. I'm Teresa. I'm one of the conference organizers.
A: Good to meet you, Teresa. I'm Ana Muñoz, from Deusto University in Spain.
T: Oh, yes, I've heard of that. Whereabouts in Spain is it?
A: In San Sebastián, in the north.
T: Oh, yes, where the Guggenheim Museum is. Fabulous building.
A: No, I think you're thinking of Bilbao. We're not a million miles from there, but it's a different branch of the university. Are you an academic, too, Teresa?
T: Yes, I lecture in social sciences at Toronto University.
A: Really? That's my field as well. Look, I'm going to get a coffee before the next session. Do you feel like joining me?
T: Yeah, that'd be great. Um ... let me just get rid of all these papers and I'll come over to the coffee area.

Conversation 2
K: Is this the right place for the bus into the city center?
J: Yes, it is. We just missed one, I'm afraid. But they come every twenty minutes. Where are you heading?
K: I've just flown in from Amman in Jordan, and now I'm going to my university accommodation.
J: OK. So, you have the address.
K: Yes.
J: Is it near the center?
K: Yes, I think so. It's on Princes Street.
J: OK. That's very central—and near the bus station. But you have a big bag, so I think your best bet would be to get a taxi when we get off. What are you going to be studying? ... Um, sorry. I didn't ask your name.
K: My name is Khalid. It's nice to meet you.
J: Hi, Khalid. Yeah, good to meet you, too. I'm Jeff, by the way. So, what are you going to be studying, Khalid?
K: I'm getting my masters in physics.
J: Wow, that sounds impressive. Way above my head, I'm afraid. .... I'm just an elementary school teacher. ... Hey, I think this is our bus now. ...

▶ 06
1 What did you think of the exhibition?
2 What kind of company is it, exactly?
3 What's it like being the only boy in a family of girls?
4 Sorry, I should have mentioned that before.
5 How are you finding the course?
6 So, have you been here before?

▶ 07
A= Antony, MA =Model answer
A: Hi there, I don't think we've met. I'm Antony.
MA: Hi, Antony. Nice to meet you. I'm José.
A: So, how do you know Nicola?
MA: We're old friends. We were at school together, actually. And you?
A: Oh. I work with Nicola's husband ... at an electronics firm. So, are you from around here?
MA: No, I live in Mexico. I'm just visiting.
A: Oh, I see. And what do you think of the city? Is it your first time here?
MA: Yes, it is. I'm really enjoying it, actually; though I have to say, I find it expensive.
A: And what have you done while you've been here? Have you been to any of the museums or anything?
MA: Not yet. I only got here two days ago. I've walked around the center a little, and I've done some sightseeing.
A: I'm supposed to take my kids on a sightseeing boat over the weekend. They've never been on one. Have you?
MA: Yes, I've been on one in Paris. But it was raining the whole time, so the views weren't great. Still, the kids will love it, I'm sure.

▶ 08

So, everyone. There have been various rumors about what paid and unpaid time off staff is entitled to, and so management would like to clarify the company's position so that everyone is clear on the situation. A short document will be sent to everyone's work email address to formalize these arrangements in a couple of weeks, but as I said, I just wanted to set the record straight now by talking to you. So, first off—sabbaticals, in other words, paid leave from work. The policy is that everyone on pay grade six or above is entitled to three months' sabbatical every six years worked. This applies only to full-time employees and not to part-time employees. Arrangements for part-time employees are being discussed, but these arrangements are to be confirmed.

Second, unpaid leave. This is purely at the discretion of your manager. He or she will decide each case on the circumstances of the employee. For example, if they have a difficult situation at home, such as sick or elderly parents. Having said that, normally no unpaid leave will be allowed for any employee who's worked at the company for less than eighteen months.

▶ 09

Now, I've called everyone here today because we're about to test out a radical new idea, which is to set no limits on how much or how little vacation each member of staff can take. That's right—no limits. Initially the company is going to try this new policy out for a limited period, in other words, just six months. That's because we're not entirely sure if it's going to work or not, but we're pretty confident it will.

What are the reasons for this policy? Well, we think that it's much better to be adult and responsible about this. We all have busy working lives with meetings to go to and targets to reach. And we all also have busy lives outside work, with families to take care of after and interests to pursue. If we're given a little freedom, we can organize our own time better.

So what are your responsibilities in this new scheme? Note that this is not an excuse to take as much time off work as possible. Nor is it something you can organize completely independently: You'll still have to negotiate with colleagues in case the timing of your vacation disrupts business in some way. You'll also still have your work targets to reach.

And finally the details. The exact start date is to be confirmed, but it will begin in the second half of this year. The policy applies to every employee including part-time staff. It will be reviewed after approximately four months. And that's it. Any questions?

Unit 2

▶ 10

Take a walk on the mountain slopes of the Tibetan Plateau in May or June, and you are likely to come across groups of people on their hands and knees, intently searching the grass for something they cannot find. It's as if someone had dropped a valuable ring, and then asked their friends and relatives to come and help them search for it.

Actually, what they're looking for is a small fungus called *yartsa gunbu* that is so prized in China for its medicinal properties that half a kilo has been known to sell for up to $50,000. Not surprising, perhaps, when you realize how difficult it is to find. One couple I talked to had been searching all day and found only thirty specimens.

Yartsa gunbu occurs in very specific conditions. Only found on the Tibetan Plateau and in the Himalayas, the mushroom is formed when the larva of a particular type of moth hatches underground and becomes infected with the fungus. As the larva grows into a caterpillar, the fungus eats it from the inside. In late spring, the fungus sends a brown stalk up through the dead caterpillar's head and out of the ground. It is this tiny stalk that the worm diggers are searching for.

For centuries, herbal doctors have prescribed *yartsa gunbu* for all sorts of medical problems: back pain, fatigue, asthma, poor eyesight. People who take it are convinced it revitalizes a person's "chi" or "life energy." Legend says that yaks that eat it grow ten times stronger. Now, with China's growing wealth, demand for *yartsa gunbu* has soared and so has the income of the locals who farm it. Thousands of poor yak herders now own motorcycles and iPhones and flat-screen TVs. Some are even more successful. Zhaxicaiji, a former yak herder, started her own *yartsa* company in 1998 and, since then, the business has grown year after year. It now has twenty stores and turnover of $60 million.

These communities are thriving on *yartsa gunbu*'s rarity. But that very rarity may also be their downfall. The harvest is currently roughly 400 million specimens, and ecologists say that if this overpicking does not stop and some stalks are not left in the ground, the cycle will stop, because the fungus that infects the larvae will have disappeared. Perhaps the next generation of golden worm diggers will be searching harder than ever.

▶ 11

/ɪ/	/iː/	/aɪ/
medicinal	previous	private
specimen	kilo	unscientific
specific	visa	survive
caterpillar		prescribe
artist		tiny
		revitalize
		financial

▶ 12

I = Interviewer, J = John
I: So, John, how did you come across this story?
J: I've been traveling in this region for many years, and I'd seen this phenomenon before but never paid much attention to it.
I: And what was it that interested you this time?
J: Well, often you'll visit a place with a particular story in mind. Then, while you're researching it,

you find something else catches your interest.

I: And what was that in this case?

J: I was very struck by how well-off people in the village seemed compared to when I'd last visited. So I decided to investigate.

▶ 13

P = Presenter, RE = Daniel Raven-Ellison

P: Could you cross a forest without touching the ground? What would you see if you walked through your entire city taking a photo every eight steps? How would it feel to locate a missing cat and return it to its owner? How far could you walk sucking on the same mint? This is geography, Daniel Raven-Ellison style. A former geography teacher, Raven-Ellison uses movies, books, websites, and walks to take geography beyond memorizing dots on a map, challenging children and adults to experience every aspect of the world around them in a more meaningful, surprising way. Here is Daniel Raven-Ellison.

RE: The internet makes us feel the world is becoming smaller and more available, but at the same time, many real, lived experiences are shrinking. For children, outdoor exploration improves mental and physical health, expands learning through risk taking, spurs innovative problem solving, and encourages empathy by meeting different people; yet too few children are allowed to play outdoors nowadays. As adults, although we share our cities with millions of other people, many of us are more disconnected than ever before, moving from the island of our home to the island of our car to the island of our office without meaningfully engaging with each other, nature, or the places in between. But for our ancestors, adventure was normal. Adventure has now become something we only watch on TV. In fact, there are amazing adventures to be had right outside our doorsteps.

P: For Raven-Ellison, this road to adventure is "guerrilla geography": asking people to challenge their preconceptions about places, engage in social and environmental justice, and form deeper community connections. His *Urban Earth* movies demonstrate guerrilla geography in action. He created them by walking across Mumbai, Mexico City, London, and ten other U.K. and U.S. cities from one extreme edge to the other, while photographing whatever lay directly in front of him every eight steps. All photos, edited together, become a movie portrait of each city. Raven-Ellison again.

RE: Travel shows and guidebooks select what they want you to see. They twist things. My movies give you an unaltered look at the reality of a city as a whole. When you're not protected by the speed or armor of a car, you see what's actually happening neighborhood by neighborhood.

P: With more than half of the world's people living in urban areas, Raven-Ellison hopes the movies will break down boundaries that isolate communities. He says that we need to engage with each other to reduce conflict, instead of being afraid to explore certain neighborhoods. Raven-Ellison's movies have inspired innovative walks for groups. He starts by handing the map to someone else. In one walk, he launched ten teams of people from different points outside London, all headed toward the city center, converging at a pub where they compared experiences and shared ideas about how to improve Britain's neighborhoods.

RE: The act of actually walking and experiencing that space gives you a different, more tangible perspective of our environmental impacts.

P: The educational project *Mission: Explore* has guerrilla geography incorporated into its children's programs. They've developed a website and series of books with hundreds of challenges that show geography's fun side, including mini field trips, neighborhood explorations, and creative science experiments. It's a hands-on format that's very accessible to children. Many of the tasks seem fun and simple but actually require high-level thinking. One challenge suggests children conduct a survey to see how friendly their community is, write to their local politicians with the findings, and offer ways the community could be improved for children. Another proposes you blindfold yourself and get a friend to help you explore by using your other senses. I'll leave you with a last word from Raven-Ellison.

RE: Memorizing things for quizzes isn't enough. Children need to have skills for interpretation, analysis, and understanding. Education can't be based just on how much you know, but must also be measured by how creative and innovative you can be. Giving children time and space to explore outdoors allows moments to happen that will be crucial for tackling issues like climate change, water shortages, and other big problems.

▶ 14

I = Interviewer, H = Hiroki Katagawa

I: So, can you tell me a little about yourself, Hiroki, and what attracted you to this graduate training program?

H: So. Um … yes, thank you. My name is Hiroki Katagawa. I'm 24 years old and I'm master … I have a master's degree in business administration. So, my first degree was in town planning, um I mean … urban planning. I spent one year in Japan working on a metro and transportation hub in the city of Osaka—it's a major city on Honshu Island. It was for work experience, and I received a kind of award when I left the project. So this is what attracted me to your company … because you are involved in such infrastructure projects.

I: And why do you think you are suited to this particular program?

H: I have good planning and organization, and up-to-date IT skills. Perhaps you would like me to give you an example. In Osaka, I helped design the program for planning work schedules for the staff working …

I: Sorry, you designed the program or you were using bespoke software?

H: I'm sorry, what?

I: Was that software you adapted or created?

H: Oh, no, it was a well-known program used in Japan, but I had to adapt it, yes … So, as I was saying, it was for planning schedules for staff working on tramlines in the city. This work had to be arranged with the consent of the local authorities, the transportation office of Osaka.

I: OK. Well, that is very relevant to what we do here …

H: And you also asked me about my suitability for this program. I am very interested in joining an international company. I am very open to different cultures, very interested in different cultures. I like travel very much and have made many friends and contacts in different countries. This is important for me—to work and live together with people from other cultures. I love to learn different approaches to life … in fact, in general I am very enthusiastic to learn.

I: OK. Thank you, Hiroki. A little earlier, we gave you a form …

▶ 16

I = Interviewer, MA = Model answer

1

I: So can you tell me a little about yourself and what attracted you to this job?

MA: Yes, my name is Eduardo Torres, and I'm a graduate in hotel management. I have been working for the last year at a small hotel in the country, and I'd like to get a job with a bigger hotel.

2

I: And what would you say your strongest qualities are?

MA: I'm well organized, and I'm good at solving problems. In fact, I love the challenge of dealing with clients' problems and trying to find the best solution.

3

I: I see. And why do you think you would be suited to this particular hotel?

MA: I know this is a prestigious international hotel, so I imagine the challenge to maintain good standards is very high.

Unit 3

▶ 17

Speaker 1

You've probably heard of Glastonbury. It's in the west of England. It's fairly well known around the world for its music festival, which is massive—over 170,000 people go each year. It takes place in the month of July on some agricultural land near the town, which is owned by a local farmer. Well, I live in the town of Glastonbury, which is not the same thing. I actually remember when it was just a small market town like others in the area: gentle countryside around it, pleasant period houses, a beautiful church, a few tea houses, and quaint shops. All in all, it was quite a sleepy, traditional kind of English town. Well, that was before Glastonbury Festival got big in the seventies and the hippies began to move in—I guess people had had such a transformative experience at the festival that they thought they'd stay to keep the magic alive somehow. Well, now the town is a rather odd mix of older, more conservative residents—I don't want to put myself in that category, mind you—and younger people who want an alternative lifestyle. So these days the High Street is full of vegetarian restaurants, second-hand music shops, bookshops that specialize in magic and ancient mysteries, shops selling healing crystals … it's all a bit wacky, really, but actually I quite like it!

Speaker 2

Ghent isn't my hometown, but it was my adopted town for a while. Actually, it might be cheating slightly to call it a town. It has around 250,000 inhabitants, which makes it more like a city, but it doesn't feel like a city because it's quite compact. They say Ghent is Belgium's best-kept secret because it's such an attractive place and yet remains relatively unknown. It doesn't get the number of visitors that Bruges or Brussels gets, which is also a bit odd because it's exactly halfway between the two. I guess part of its charm is that it's so many things rolled into one: It's a university town, a historic town, a port, an industrial town. So on one hand, it feels a little like a working town because of the industry around the old docks: There's a huge steel mill, a truck assembly plant, Europe's biggest fruit juice terminal ... they say. But on the other hand, if you don't see that part, it seems like a well-preserved historic town. I was a student there, and I had an amazing time. It was really lively and friendly. One of the benefits of having that kind of mix—I mean, old and new, academic and industrial—is that people tend to be quite open-minded and accepting. There's also lots to do—a good music scene, interesting museums and galleries, beautiful architecture, nice parks—but going out isn't particularly cheap. The other drawback is the weather, which is pretty terrible most of the time—gray and rainy. I'm from Italy, and I have to say, it got me down a bit at times.

▶ 19

A: How was your trip to Russia?

B: Great, thanks. We had a fairly packed schedule, but it was very interesting. We started in Moscow and saw the sights around Red Square. Strangely, the thing I loved most was the subway. Each station is like a work of art in itself. The service is pretty efficient, too.

A: And how did it compare to St. Petersburg?

B: Very different. St. Petersburg is a very grand and gracious city. Actually, it feels a bit closer in atmosphere to other cities in central Europe, whereas Moscow doesn't feel particularly European. But that's the thing about Russia. You don't realize what an enormous and diverse country it is until you travel there.

21

J = Jim, K = Kirsten Sommer

J: So I'm here with architectural historian Kirsten Sommer to talk about the subject of biomimetics and why it's relevant to architecture today. Kirsten, biomimetics—which I should explain to any listeners who are not familiar with the term—is the idea of copying good design from nature and applying it to things that are human-made. It's something I associate more with material science and robotics, and things like that. But I think you've found strong evidence of it in the history of architecture, too.

K: Yes, hello, Jim, that's right. But first of all, I think we should be careful perhaps about how we label these things. We need to separate the term *biomimetics*, which was coined in the 1950s, from the practice of simply taking inspiration from nature's forms, which is obviously a much older phenomenon. The term *biomimetics* is now used for the development of new technologies—like human-made fibers that can imitate the properties of duck feathers, or high-tech swimsuits that replicate shark skin. A classic example of it is Velcro, which imitates barbs on the head of a thistle plant. But for a long time—and still very much today—architects have taken inspiration from the forms and shapes of nature.

J: Can you give us an example?

K: Yes, um … probably the best known building of this kind is Gaudí's Sagrada Familia in Barcelona …

J: That's not even finished yet, is it?

K: No. Its history is complicated, but before his death in 1926, Gaudí left very clear instructions—in the form of three-dimensional models—as to how he'd like it finished. The date for completion is now 2026. But anyway, Gaudí loved nature and understood that the natural world is full of curved forms, not straight lines. So with organic models in mind and the materials that nature uses to create its structures: wood, muscle, tendon, etc., he created a very organic-looking building in the Sagrada Familia, an architectural form that borrowed from nature in a way that no one had seen before.

J: It is, or certainly was, a controversial building, wasn't it?

K: Oh, absolutely. It's one of those buildings that people either love or hate. George Orwell called it "one of the most hideous buildings in the world." Others, like the surrealists, loved its originality. Gaudí's own explanation for its originality was that it had "returned to the origin"; in other words, it was original in the sense that it had gone back to nature.

J: And who is using biomimetics these days in architecture?

K: Oh, my goodness, there are so many examples. You only have to look at the names of buildings to tell you that: The Swiss Re Tower in London is known as the "Gherkin"; the Olympic stadium in Beijing, which people called the "Bird's Nest"; Frank Gehry's "Fish" in Barcelona. But it's about more than just the external shape and appearance of buildings. Architects are using biomimetics to create more environmentally friendly buildings.

J: Yes, I read about the Eastgate Centre in Harare being innovative in that way.

K: Yes, that's a very good example. It's not only unusual to look at—modern office and shopping complexes are typically all steel and glass these days. What's more interesting is the use of chimneys to imitate the heating and cooling system in a termite mound. It's called passive cooling, and it's very energy efficient and does away with the need for a modern air-conditioning system. It works by storing heat that is generated inside the building in the walls and then letting this heat escape through the chimneys at night, so the building is nice and cool the following morning.

22

A: Well, first of all, I should say that I think it's basically a good idea—it has a lot of things to recommend it: principally, that people won't have to waste time going down to the cafeteria to get their coffee. Also, it'll encourage employee interaction, which of course is a good thing. But I have to say there's a risk in that, because if you make an area that's too comfortable or convivial, they might spend just as much time there as they did going down to the cafeteria—in other words, away from productive work.

B: I kind of disagree with that. The thing about an open-plan office is that it feels rather large and impersonal, and so the idea of putting in some area that feels more intimate really appeals to me. I think you have to be careful about terms like *productive work*. You said yourself that employee interaction was something to be encouraged, and I think that can take different forms—from formal meetings to informal chats. The informal chats are something we shouldn't underestimate the importance of. What I mean is, if we assume that people relaxing and having coffee at work are wasting the company's time, then for me that is a sad state of affairs. So I'm very much in favor of this proposal, particularly given that we are all working in a rather impersonal environment, as I said before. Oh, and by the way, including a screen with industry news on it in the room is a nice touch.

C = Colleague, MA = Model answer

1

C: Would you prefer to have a large living space or somewhere that's small and cozy?

MA: Personally, I'd like to have a lot of space, but maybe that seems a bit selfish. After all, it's not a choice everyone can make.

2

C: Do you think that the architecture around you affects how you are feeling?

MA: Yes, I think it probably does. Not consciously maybe, but I don't think you should underestimate its impact.

3

C: I've heard it said that 80 percent of people end up living no more than 30 kilometers from where they were born. I think that's a rather surprising statistic.

MA: Do you? I disagree. I think most people like to stay near their family and friends. And also it's pretty clear that the bond that we form with our surroundings as we grow up is very strong.

4

C: I don't think there's enough new and radical design in architecture. There is for a few people who are prepared to pay for it, but most new buildings are just boring.

MA: I agree completely. A lot of new buildings either copy existing designs or go for the cheapest design. I'm in favor of people trying out new things, and I don't think new always means more expensive.

Unit 4

▶ 28

There are three things you can do when you meet a physical obstacle—go around it, go over it, or go under it. Now, imagine that physical obstacle is the traffic in our cities. We've already tried going around it by building bypass roads around our cities, but actually, such solutions are never likely to work because just as new channels around a sandcastle on the beach fill with water, so new roads fill with cars as soon as you build them.

That leaves two options: to build new traffic systems in the air or underground. But either way, rather than removing the problem, you might just be moving it somewhere else. The problem with the former is that collisions or accidents in the air could also have an impact on those below when debris falls from a height. The problem with the latter has always been the expense.

Until now, that is, because American entrepreneur Elon Musk thinks he has an answer. And given his amazing record of not only finding but also implementing innovative solutions, there's a good chance that he could pull this off.

His latest venture, The Boring Company, proposes building a network of tunnels under cities that transports vehicles on high-speed electric sleds. The key to making this happen will be speeding up the tunneling process and making it a lot cheaper. Musk's idea is that by using smaller single-lane tunnels and more efficient boring or tunneling machines, his techniques should reduce the cost enormously. Vehicles would then travel down each tunnel at high speeds and only in one direction, so that there would be nothing to block them or hold them up. In his

mind, also, is the idea that in the future, the tunnels will possibly use vacuum technology, in which pods carrying cars can travel at speeds of up to 900 kilometers per hour. This technology, part of Musk's so-called Hyperloop project, has already been tried and tested in California.

▶ 30

H = Host, F = Freya Wint

H: Philanthropy is back in fashion—some say in the United States it never went out of fashion. Now a new generation of internet and mobile communications billionaires are supporting good causes like never before. The difference is that so many more of these do-gooders are self-made businessmen and women, whereas in the past they were individuals who relied on inherited wealth. Are there other differences between these philanthropists and their 19th-century counterparts? I put this question to social historian Freya Wint.

F: Very definitely. The philanthropists of the 19th century tended to set up long-term foundations and scholarships so that their legacies would benefit future generations. What you have now is a number of people—Bill Gates being the most famous—who have made money relatively quickly in their lifetime and are now actively involved in doing good with it … and enjoying themselves. "Giving while living" is the slogan.

H: And is there a difference in the way they give?

F: Oh, certainly. Because they are more hands-on, they are also more concerned about seeing the short-term benefits to what they are doing. In many cases, they treat their giving in much the same way as they treat their other business investments; they even describe their programs in business terms like "getting a good return on capital," "making stakeholders accountable," and "setting agreed and measurable targets." The money they put into philanthropic projects is like seed money—they want to see the projects grow and prosper by themselves, become self-sustaining eventually.

H: Do you have any concrete examples of that?

F: Yes, a good example is Jeff Skoll, the Canadian founder of eBay, which is the world's largest online marketplace. He set up something called the Skoll Foundation, which supports and promotes social entrepreneurship. The foundation aims to identify people and ideas that are already helping bring about positive change in areas where social problems exist. I was particularly struck reading about one of the entrepreneurs he backed, a woman named Daniela Papi. She used to run voluntourism projects in Cambodia, where volunteers paid to come and help build schools there. But she soon realized that a more long-term and sustainable approach would be to promote teacher training and curriculum development in the schools. Then she realized that in these volunteers that came on her program, there was great potential … for them to go to other places and bring about positive change there. So now she focuses on that aspect, too. I just thought that was a great example of how a little money behind the right person can develop into a much wider benefit, and I think that's what today's philanthropists are all about.

H: So is there none of the old-fashioned "no strings attached" kind of giving anymore?

F: Oh, no … there are still a lot of donations—rather than investments—made to people who are in a bad situation and can't help themselves—medicine for HIV sufferers, of water and food supplies for those who have been hit by drought or famine. John Caudwell, the man who made his fortune in the cell phone business, gives most of his money to disabled children. He's a self-confessed capitalist who believes in people helping themselves, but he recognizes that there are some people who aren't born lucky like him. Essentially, by providing them with wheelchairs or walking aids, he's giving them greater independence and opportunity. I'd say that was very typical of the ethos of the new philanthropists. There's more emphasis on self-help than with former philanthropists.

H: It must make them feel good, too.

F: Oh, absolutely. No one wants to be remembered only as the person who made a billion selling phones or laptops—they want to be remembered for the contribution they made to making the world a better place.

▶ 31

We have designed a school bag for children. What's so original about that, you ask? Well, this is a bag that also functions as a desk. So you can fold it out and work at it, anytime and anywhere you like. Why would children want to do that, when they have a desk at school and a table at home? Well, simply because not all children do have a desk at school or even a table at home. I'd like you to stop and just think about that for a minute. Our ambition for this school bag is that it will not only be used by children in Europe but also in developing countries. Because that is where it will really come into its own. It has numerous compartments for notebooks, pens, and a water holder. Hydration, as you know, is very important for concentration. But how will people in poorer countries be able to afford the bag? Well, that's why we call it the Solidarity Bag. Because we're setting the price a little higher here in Europe to help lower the cost of a bag for a family in a developing country. So when you pay 35 euros for the bag here, you are helping bring the price down to an affordable level elsewhere, showing solidarity with families less fortunate than you.

▶ 33

I = Investor, MA = Model answer

1
I: Can you just explain to me what your ambition is for this product?

MA: Yes. We would like it to have successful sales in Europe and on the basis of that to be able to provide many of these bags to children in developing countries.

2
I: And do you think that customers will support this ambition?

MA: Yes, I think that it's very important for people nowadays to feel they can do some good when they buy things. People want ethical products.

3
I: But the price of the bag is pretty high for European customers.

MA: It is high, but it is a good-quality bag and I think people are prepared to pay a little extra for an ethical product.

4
I: And do you think the fact that it can also function as a desk is useful for children in Europe?

MA: It's not as useful as it is for children in some developing countries. But I think it is a feature that they will enjoy, and it might encourage them to work in places where they didn't before.

5
I: And if we invest, what will you use the money for?

MA: The most important thing for us is to make people aware of the Solidarity Bag. We will invest in an advertising and publicity campaign.

Unit 5

▶ 34

Maybe like me, you're one of those people who used to look at organized tours and think: "never in a million years!" Why would I want to be herded around like a sheep with a group of people I've never met before, tied to a strict schedule, and taken to all the obvious tourist places rather than the more undiscovered ones? What I want from travel is a little independence.

Well, that's what I *used* to think. And the thing that changed my mind was a guided tour I took at the Metropolitan Museum of Art in New York. I was in New York on vacation and it was raining hard, so I dived into the museum to escape the rain. Don't get me wrong—I do like visiting museums; this just happened to be an unplanned visit. So I wandered over to the information desk and asked what was on, and they said that, among other things, there was a tour of the museum's early Christian art collection and it was going to begin in a few minutes. OK, I thought to myself, it'll be an experience, if nothing else. So, not holding out much hope, I joined it. Well, it *was* an experience—a really *good* one. Because rather than wander around the museum looking at 200 objects and not really taking in any of them properly, as I would normally have done, we were shown by this incredibly knowledgeable guide just a small number of … maybe five or six really interesting artifacts. She explained the story and context behind each one in lots of detail—and it was fascinating. The experience didn't quite inspire me to want to become an expert on early Christian art, but it did make me reassess my whole attitude toward organized tours.

A year later, I went on a guided trip to Italy. Again, the guides were brilliant—mostly qualified archeologists and historians. You know, to get that much information about somewhere, you'd have to do weeks, probably months, of reading beforehand. What surprised me, too, was how knowledgeable and interesting some of the other travelers were—not the sheep I'd ignorantly thought they'd be before …

There are lots of other benefits, too. Your transportation, hotel, food: It's all taken care of; all the visits are pre-arranged, so you don't have to book anything. The convenience factor is *not* to be underestimated, like particularly if it's a more remote or not-so-safe place you're visiting. Imagine all the pressure and anxiety from planning and booking and missed connections that it cuts out. It's so liberating.

And, talking of liberating, what about free time? It's actually a myth that organized tours are too regimented—in fact, they've always factored in free time for people to go off and explore by themselves, and these days they're even more sensitive to that than ever. A lot of operators offer you the option of not going on excursions if you'd prefer to make your own itinerary.

▶ 35
1   I do wish I had been able to spend more time there.
2   He did say that he'd help us.
3   We do prefer to take vacations close to home.
4   She does get very sunburned.

▶ 37
1   Would you like to come to dinner some evening?
2   Do you need to borrow a pen?
3   Are you coming?
4   I didn't get the assistant manager job.
5   Are you going away this summer?
6   Do you like detective stories?
7   What are you doing here so early?

▶ 38
I've been on a few mystery tours, but the one I did in Prague was probably the best. And I'm not the only person to say so. If you look at reviews, you'll hardly find one negative one. I'm not going to give you too many details because that would spoil the surprise if one day you happened to do it, too. What I will tell you is that it started at night and involved a segway, some canoes, a jazz band, and a large breakfast. If that hasn't aroused your curiosity, I don't know what will!

▶ 39
Now when I was young, I had a passion for maps. I would look for hours at South America, or Africa, or Australia, and lose myself in all the glories of exploration. At that time, there were many blank spaces on Earth, and when I saw one that looked particularly inviting on a map (but they all look that),

I would put my finger on it and say, "When I grow up, I will go there." The North Pole was one of these places, I remember. Well, I haven't been there yet, and won't try now. The glamour is gone. Other places were scattered about the hemispheres. I have been in some of them, and … well, we won't talk about that. But there was one yet—the biggest, the most blank, so to speak—that I had a hankering after.

True, by this time, it was not a blank space anymore. It had gotten filled since my boyhood with rivers and lakes and names. It had ceased to be a blank space of delightful mystery—a white patch for a boy to dream gloriously over. It had become a place of darkness. But there was in it one river especially, a mighty big river, that you could see on the map, resembling an immense snake uncoiled, with its head in the sea, its body at rest curving afar over a vast country, and its tail lost in the depths of the land. And as I looked at the map of it in a shop window, it fascinated me as a snake would a bird—a silly little bird. Then I remembered there was a company for trade on that river. Dash it all! I thought to myself, they can't trade without using some kind of craft on that lot of fresh water—steamboats! Why shouldn't I try to get charge of one?
I went on along Fleet Street, but could not shake off the idea. The snake had charmed me.

I got my appointment—of course; and I got it very quick. It appears the company had received news that one of their captains had been killed in a scuffle with the natives. Soon after I left in a French steamer, and she called in every port they have out there. I watched the coast. Watching a coast as it slips by the ship is like thinking about an enigma. There it is before you—smiling or frowning, grand or mean, insipid or savage, and always mute with an air of whispering, "Come and find out." This one was almost featureless, with an aspect of monotonous grimness. The edge of a colossal jungle, so dark-green as to be almost black, fringed with white surf, ran straight, like a ruled line, far, far away along a blue sea.

▶ 40
Very few people still hitchhike these days. We all know that it can be dangerous. And actually, why would you take the risk when there are so many other cheap options available, like buses? But if you have the time—and that's important 'cause it's generally not a quick way to travel—if you have the time, you *can* have some amazing experiences. A year ago, a group of us from our university had a competition to see who could get to Los Angeles the quickest by hitchhiking. We were in pairs, and we all set off from different points in Denver. Amazingly, within about ten minutes, we got a ride with a truck driver. We couldn't believe our luck. We drove for about six hours, and then around midnight, the driver said he had to stop to get some sleep. He pulled over at a rest stop, which, by chance, happened to have an area for pitching tents. Thinking it would be better not to disturb him, we got out and put up our little tent.

The following morning, we woke up early, ready to

get back in the truck, but to our dismay, it had left. We sat down and tried to rationalize the situation: He'd probably just had an emergency and couldn't help leaving in a hurry; we'd probably get another ride before too long—if anyone else stopped here—but the place was actually deserted. Feeling pretty miserable, we started to pack up our tent. But just at that moment, we heard a loud honking. It was our driver. He pulled up, jumped out of the truck, and produced three cups of coffee and some fresh donuts.

▶ 41

Long vowel sound: amazement, delight, dismay, frustration, relief, surprise

Short vowel sound: astonishment, embarrassment, horror, regret, shock, consequence

▶ 42

F = Friend, MA = Model answer
F: So, tell me what happened.
M: Well, a couple of weeks ago, I took the train to go and visit my aunt in Newville.
F: And what went wrong?
M: I was really tired because I had been up late the night before and I started to doze.
F: Did you wake up in time for your stop?
M: No, I woke up just as the train was leaving Newville, and the next station was fifty kilometers away.
F: Oh, no! What did you do?
M: Well, luckily, there was a really nice conductor on the train. And he explained to me the quickest way to get back to my station from the next stop. He also put a note on my ticket saying I didn't need to pay again.

Unit 6

▶ 43

In 1968, the Beatles turned up in Rishikesh, India, to study transcendental meditation at Maharishi Mahesh Yogi's ashram. They wrote about forty songs here, many of which ended up on their famous *White Album*. I hadn't come to write music, but to get over chronic back pain—one of my vertebrae being severely out of line—or at least put off the day when I would have to face back surgery.

Perched above the Ganges River, Rishikesh is now a shopping mall for those looking for mental and physical healing, pulling in hundreds of thousands of foreign visitors each year. My chosen retreat was the Parmarth Niketan Ashram, which is less strict than other ashrams and allows guests to come and go as they please. I had also been attracted by the fact that it supports around 200 disadvantaged boys—some orphaned—putting them up in simple accommodations, and providing them with food, and a basic education.

At 6:50 a.m. on the first day, I found myself sitting in a plain room with a wooden floor, white walls, and a metal roof. We worked on a breathing technique that involved inhaling and exhaling through one nostril

at a time. There were no other distractions—no New Age tunes playing, no yoga outfits, no blinding heat, no incense, and no attitude; just students and a teacher. Meals were conducted in silence, something that I found odd at first but came to appreciate. During one of the meals, another guest sitting across the 20-centimeter-high table broke this silence to comment on how horribly fast I ate. I felt a little taken aback, but thanked him and noted the point.

The yoga carried on in a serene way for two weeks, never causing me even to break a sweat. In fact, more than once I wondered how it could be helping me. Yet by the end of my visit, the simple lessons—stretch, breathe, eat more slowly and more healthily, relax—had an effect. I can now touch my toes and even sit cross-legged for thirty minutes through a meal. My back? The persistent pain hasn't entirely gone away, but it has subsided. More importantly, I can now put up with it because I've given up worrying about it.

▶ 44

A: The other day I looked up what fitness classes there were available locally, and I couldn't believe how many there were.
B: Did you come across any that you liked the look of?
A: Not really. I didn't know what half of them were: Boxercise, Boot camp, Aqua aerobics … and lots based on dance.
B: You mean like Zumba?
A: Yes. I knew Zumba was a craze that had taken off, but there were others: Jazzercise, Bodyjam. I mean, if you like dancing, why don't you just sign up for a dance class?
B: And do you? Like dancing, that is?
A: Yes, I do. I think that's what I'll do … take up samba or something.

▶ 46

I = Interviewer, E = Expert
I: What impact has globalization had on our idea of beauty?
E: Well, I guess the first thing to say is that not necessarily globalization, but general economic growth, has had a huge impact on the amount of time and money people spend on beautification. The global cosmetics and perfume industry is worth around $200 billion. Americans spend over a billion each year on their fingernails alone. And new markets keep being found. Male grooming, which twenty years ago was not a big industry at all, now brings in over $30 billion. But I think the question you're getting at is: Has a globalized world made our ideal of beauty more homogenized?
I: Yes, I suppose what I'm asking is: Is there now a more global view of what beautiful is or means?
E: Well, that's an interesting question and I think the beauty industry is a good example of what has happened more generally in the world over the last one hundred years or so. But I think we need to stress that there have been different stages of globalization—not just the most recent one that

began in the 1980s. If you go back to the early 20th century and the days of Western imperialism, you do find that cosmetics companies were peddling a Western and "white" ideal of beauty. There was even the promise by some companies that regular washing with soap could help to turn a dark skin whiter.

I: Goodness!

E: Obviously, it was an effective marketing tactic: If people everywhere could aspire to the same notion of beauty, it would be far easier for the companies to mass-produce products. So, using the ideals presented by Hollywood movie stars and fashion magazines, they persuaded people not only that it was desirable to look a certain way, but that their collection of skin creams and lipsticks and fragrances would help them achieve that.

I: And did that marketing effort really work? Were people convinced by these ideas of beauty?

E: Well, yes and no. Local cultural values were never completely taken over by the global message of the marketers. People aren't stupid, and they could see that they were being offered an American ideal. Henry Kissinger was right when he said that globalization in that era was just another name for Americanization. You know, I think generally people are able to differentiate between what they are being asked to aspire to and the reality of their daily lives.

I: And you talked about different eras of globalization. Can you just explain a bit more about that?

E: Sure. Well, the more recent era of globalization—the one that began in the 1980s—is one in which companies definitely have to be more conscious of local traditions and values. You only have to look at how a company like McDonald's alters its menu to suit the tastes of each local market to see that. There is an increasing emphasis on diversity. So, as we all seem to get closer in a world of global communications, at the same time, we want to celebrate individuality and local differences.

I: So now companies incorporate diversity into the products they make?

E: Definitely. Multinational companies can still accept the universal values of beauty that we all aspire to: a clear skin, healthy-looking hair, a youthful glow, and then they can adapt their products to include local and traditional ingredients: for example, black soap in Africa for skin cleansing, or the Huito fruit in South America—traditionally used for body painting—as an ingredient in hair dye.

▶ 47

Speaker 1
On the whole, I really like what the architect's done. But he's put in two elevators, which I think is excessive. A better alternative would be to have just one, which can be a service elevator and also be used for wheelchair access. That way, people will be obliged to use the stairs—it's only two flights—and

that will actually be good for them. It'll help them stay fit. I realize that sometimes people who have heavy things to move or who aren't so mobile will sometimes want to use the elevator, but we can easily work around that.

Speaker 2
I think the health problems associated with air-conditioning systems are well documented. What you're getting is the same air—and so consequently the same germs and diseases—being recycled around the building. It would be much better just to have straightforward fresh air sucked in from outside, as Giovanni suggests. Admittedly, it wouldn't always be cool air, but it would be a lot healthier.

Speaker 3
I think the idea of a staff cafeteria is great, but we have to be very careful who we choose to run it. I think what we need to do is to make up our own list of what kind of food we think is acceptable—healthy options and so on—and then invite local companies to bid for the contract. I haven't really thought through who should be responsible for making the list, but I do think it's important to make one.

Speaker 4
I think the idea of forming a partnership with the local fitness and leisure center is probably the best option. I love the idea of staff being able to do sports together—it'd be very good for morale. I know not everyone will want to join in in that way, but for a lot of people, the social element will really be a big attraction.

▶ 49

C = Colleague, MA = Model answer
1
C: What do you think of the proposal?
MA: I think it's a great idea. It would really help staff to keep in shape and get exercise during their lunch hour or after work.
2
C: And do you think that staff will really make good use of it?
MA: I don't see why not. Admittedly, there will be some who aren't interested, but I think that they'll be the minority.
3
C: Don't you think that it's an expensive way to promote health among the staff?
MA: Well, I realize it's not going to be cheap, but I think that you have to look at all the benefits—like reducing the number of days of absence and making people more productive.
4
C: And do you see other benefits, too?
MA: Well, yes. I think it could help attract people to come and work for us. It's a good advertisement for the company.

Unit 7

▶ 50

There's a paradox about technology. It's generally thought to be a positive thing, something that solves problems and helps us be healthier and live more comfortably. But at the same time, it's also created a lot of problems for our planet: Emissions from industrial plants are changing our atmosphere, and plastic debris in our oceans is believed to be changing marine ecosystems irreparably as we speak.

So I was fascinated to read the other day about a use of new technology that combines exploration with conservation. An archeologist named Albert Yu-Min Lin is doing archeology in a kind of virtual reality way. Working with the California Institute for Telecommunications and Information Technology, Lin has swapped his shovel and trowel for an array of digital 3D immersive technologies.

What this allows him to do is to gather, synthesize, and visualize data using cutting-edge tools such as satellite imagery and ground-penetrating radar. This means he can make discoveries in areas where physical excavations would be either physically difficult or highly sensitive.

One example is the search for the tomb of Genghis Khan, a quest that is known to have frustrated scientists and historians for centuries. For many Mongolians, the tomb is considered to be an extremely sacred place and it's even said by some that disturbing it could trigger a curse that would end the world.

But most impressive are the labs where all this data is crunched—the Star Cave. The Star Cave is a totally immersive virtual reality room where scientists and historians can navigate, fly, and manipulate their way through landscapes. Backlit screens project images on the ground and walls, and special eyewear creates the 3D effect. Virtual explorers zoom over mountains, down slopes. So when Lin learns from an ancient text where a particular mountain or tomb was supposed to have been in the past, he can go into the Star Cave and travel around that region to find evidence of its existence.

At the moment, these new approaches are being used by archeologists, historians, and geologists, but they are expected to benefit all kinds of projects in the future, from tracking animal migrations to mapping the brain. The principle of synthesizing information gathered using digital technology and then creating a new 3D world remains the same.

▶ 51

I was very aware during my travels across Europe, posting my blog and photos, that Paris was going to present a particular challenge. I didn't want to photograph the obvious sites, like the Eiffel Tower, even though I was interested in visiting them all. But as Paris is said to be one of the world's most photogenic cities, instead, I decided to take as few images as possible and come away with some really memorable compositions.

So here they are. They're not supposed to be anything more than a small collection of my memories of this wonderful place: more like postcards than photos.

▶ 52

P = Presenter, A = Amrita Dall

Part 1

P: … and later we'll be talking to Mr. Dearman about his ingenious new method for storing wrong-time electricity using cryogenics. But first a report from Amrita Dall, who last week visited the Cleanweb Hackathon in New York City, to learn about some exciting projects in the field of sustainability. Hi, Amrita. Just before we get into the detail of the event you visited, could you just explain to our listeners what a hackathon is?

A: Sure. It's sometimes also called a hack-day or a hackfest, but basically a hackathon is an event where computer programmers and web experts come together to design new software or new apps. They usually take place over a day or a weekend and at the end, the different teams present what they've come up with.

P: Are they competitions?

A: They often are, but they don't have to be. They're generally centered around a particular cause or a particular need, which was the case with the one I visited, the Cleanweb Hackathon in New York.

P: OK, so let's hear about that …

A: Well, I'd just better explain what Cleanweb is, then. It's a network of concerned people who are dedicated to finding what are called "cleantech" solutions to the various grave environmental problems that are facing us in the world today. What does that mean? Well, it means applying technology—web, mobile, social media technology—to the task of conserving resources, minimizing pollution, creating cleaner fuels, reducing waste, and so on.

P: And can you give an example of how those kinds of digital technology can do that?

A: Sure. One interesting idea I heard was about using social and mobile media to encourage less ownership and more efficient consumption. So, for example, you could set up a local neighborhood network on the web—a "resource cloud" as it was called—so that if one neighbor needed a tool, like an electric drill, to do a job, he or she could send that request out to the community and someone would lend one rather than the person having to buy a new one.

Part 2

P: OK. That's interesting. So are they mostly community-based ideas and not for profit?

A: No, Cleanweb definitely backs people who have good business ideas as well. One of the organizers I talked to was clear about the part that business had to play. What he said really rang true: that most people have a kind of blind faith that humanity will innovate its way out of a future environmental crisis. But actually, we're in a crisis now, and so according to him, firms and others had better start innovating now.

P: And what about the hackathon itself? Did it seem to be a good environment for serious innovation?

A: Yeah, it was a very dynamic and positive kind of atmosphere. The theme was energy, and it kicked off on Friday evening with some introductions and then sharing ideas for apps to promote energy saving and energy awareness. Then on Saturday, the various teams got down to the job of designing their apps. Work went on at a really high intensity through to Sunday when each app was submitted to the judges.

P: And who were the winners?

A: Well, one was an app called Econofy and that enabled the user, when shopping, to make comparisons between the energy efficiency of different electrical appliances. I thought that was practical, and some of the sponsors and other companies that were present were clearly very interested in it.

P: And did you get the feeling that Cleanweb could make more than just a marginal difference?

A: Yes, I really think it's an organization that could. Actually, it's wrong to call Cleanweb an "organization." It's more like a movement … and it's growing very fast: there are plans for hackathons in Italy and Canada, for example.

P: Well, thanks, Amrita. If you're now interested in getting involved in the Cleanweb network, their internet address is cleanweb.com and you …

▶ 53
See Part 1 of ▶ 52

▶ 54
See Part 2 of ▶ 52

▶ 55
A new study has detected a species of flesh-ripping dinosaur previously unknown to scientists, which is believed to have terrorized North Africa some 95 million years ago.

The species—Sauroniops pachytholus—was identified from a single fossil unearthed in southeastern Morocco in 2007 by a team of scientists led by Andrea Cau of the Bologna Geological Museum.

The fossil comprises only the upper part of the dinosaur's skull, but from this, Cau has been able to conclude that this was probably a large two-legged meat-eater rather like Tyrannosaurus rex and perhaps measuring as much as twelve meters in length. The long shape of the skull suggests that Sauroniops had a large jaw with dozens of bladelike teeth.

The fossil also revealed a large bump on Sauroniops's already thick forehead, from which it appears that this dinosaur used its head in fights with other large dinosaurs.

This fossil find reinforces the case that this area

of North Africa seems to have been particularly popular with predatory dinosaurs. Such dinosaurs tended to gather where there was an abundance of food, and the warm climate and large river delta would certainly have attracted fish and crocodiles. But whether they fought each other, as the adventure movies like to show, is another matter. Arguably, says Cau, they targeted different prey and had no need to compete for food.

▶ 57
F = Friend, MA = Model answer
1
F: So what did you find?
MA: It seems to be some kind of old oil lamp.
2
F: How do you know that's what it is?
MA: Well, it looks like the kind of lamps I've seen in museums.
3
F: How old do you think it is?
MA: Well, I couldn't say for sure, but probably it dates back to Roman times.
4
F: Do you know that that kind of object existed then?
MA: Yes, the Romans were believed to have settled in this area, so I think it's likely that it is a Roman lamp.
5
F: Do you think it has some historical significance?
MA: Well, there's some writing on the bottom of it, which suggests it could be of interest to a museum or historian.

Unit 8

▶ 58
NGM = Nat Geo Music, JS = Jake Shimabukuro
NGM: When did you first start playing the ukulele?
JS: We learned the ukulele in school like most kids learned the recorder in school. I remember when my mom first placed it in my hands and taught me my first three chords, and I was just hooked. I would play all the time. The ukulele is synonymous with Hawaii, and if you walk around Waikiki, you'll always see people hanging around playing.
NGM: What kind of music did you enjoy playing growing up in Hawaii?
JS: Up until my early teens, I was playing a lot of traditional Hawaiian music. Once I entered high school, you start meeting all these different cliques and people start introducing you to different styles of music. From classical, to jazz, to rock, and of course the popular groups on the radio at that time. So I would try and find the notes on the ukulele. People'd look at me and say, "You're not supposed to be doing that on a ukulele!" and I remember that feeling of just surprising people with doing different things. I basically created my own technique and ways of playing the instrument. I remember playing "More Than Words" by

Extreme, and everyone just freaked out! They never thought a song like that was possible to play on the ukulele.

I realize that cover songs work so well on the ukulele because it has a very limited range, which allows you to simplify the songs, since you can only play four notes at once. But the audience has such a strong reference of the tune, they're filling in the parts that can't be played on the ukulele.

NGM: What has it been like for you touring on a global scale?

JS: People always say music is the universal language, but I believe music is the language of the universe; because it communicates raw human emotion. And to me, that's more powerful than anything else. It's a more intimate, deeper connection than just having a conversation with someone.

NGM: You are quoted as saying: "If everyone played the ukulele, the world would be a better place." Why?

JS: When you have the opportunity to create music yourself, you feel more connected to the things around you. People shouldn't be intimidated by it; my grandmother just started playing it! She and her friends sit around and play, and have a blast with it. I believe just taking that step to give any kind of instrument a try will bring people immense joy. In this day and age we live in, where technology always expects us to multitask and give up our contemplative time, we're always expected to respond so quickly; it can be stressful. So coming home after a long day, picking up the ukulele, and playing it feels like a yoga session to me! It gives you the chance to let loose and act silly!

▶ 59

1 A: Should we go?
   B: Yes, I'm just coming.
2 A: How are you doing?
   B: Just fine, thanks.
3 A: Can I help you?
   B: No, thanks, I'm just looking.
4 A: Why do you ask?
   B: I'm just curious.
5 A: Is Jaz there?
   B: No. He just left.

▶ 60

Is there a way to learn an instrument fast? What do you think? The answer is almost certainly not, if you want to do it properly. To do anything well takes time and patience. You can take shortcuts to avoid learning each step, but in the end, this will catch up with you. You may reach a certain destination faster, but it won't be the one that you're ultimately aiming for. I always advise people to bear in mind the three "P"s: pay attention to your instructor; practice—to improve, you need to practice as often as possible; and patience. Progress is always slower at first, and ninety percent of people give up within the first year of taking up an instrument.

▶ 61

Ask someone to name a famous blues artist and you'll get some different names: B.B. King, Ella Fitzgerald, John Lee Hooker, but very seldom will you hear the name of the harmonica, or blues harp, genius, Sonny Boy Williamson II. Yet Sonny Boy was perhaps the first black media star of the American South. His fifteen-minute midday show on KFFA radio in the early 1940s, broadcast when workers took their main meal of the day between long shifts, was the most listened-to musical event in the Mississippi Delta at the time. It's said that on a warm summer day with the windows open, you could walk from one side of Helena, Arkansas, to the other through black and white sections of town and never miss a note of Sonny Boy's playing.

Sonny Boy Williamson was born in 1912, the youngest of twenty-one children and the only musician in the family. He started playing the harp at a young age, perhaps as early as five. He became so skilled at it that later he developed a technique where he could put the harmonica in his mouth and play without using his hands. Very little is known about his early life, but we know times were hard for black people in that era, working for little pay in factories and on the plantations, and it's from tales of hard times that the blues draws its name.

Although married, he led a rootless existence. We have accounts of him drifting around the Mississippi Delta in the 1930s captivating people with his music and jamming with other musicians in this golden era of blues music. He took himself where his music led him, up to Detroit, to Tennessee, and in the 1950s, to Chicago, where his Chess record label was based and where he made some of his greatest recordings.

What is it that sets Sonny Boy apart? His music is uncomplicated yet powerful, switching from a simple rhythm to an impassioned solo; his lyrics are moody and at the same time witty; his lyrics are delivered in a weary tone but without any sense of negativity. Above all, he's his own man, a figure who, without trying at all, exudes charisma. It's the charisma of a musical genius who is supremely confident in his art.

In the 1960s, he went to Europe to tour and was greeted wherever he went with great acclaim. It was at this time that he met various young British musicians who were influenced by American blues music. One of these was Jimmy Page, later of the rock band Led Zeppelin. Their first encounter in a nightclub says much about Sonny Boy's charisma. After seeing him play, Page approached him and said how much he admired him and enjoyed his music. Would it be all right to have his autograph? Sonny Boy gave him a withering look and told him to "get lost." Page says that he would never think of treating a fan like that himself, but there was something about Sonny Boy that made Page respect him even more. In spite of his gruff manner, Sonny Boy loved the respect he was given in Europe. One of his last recordings, made with Jimmy Page on guitar, was entitled "I'm Trying to Make London My Home."

Sonny Boy returned home but died in 1965 at the modest age of 53, when he was still at the peak of his powers. Some say he looked closer to 70. He is a legend among those who listen to the blues, and I firmly believe that one day his recordings will be appreciated by more than just a few aficionados.

▶ 62

I = Interviewer, A = Aleah

I: So you came from a very musical background. Your father was a musician and your aunt was a famous singer, too. Was it obvious to you that you'd go into music as a profession?

A: No, I never really thought about it like that. I think people suppose that I'm part of some musical dynasty—that I was destined to be a musician. But my mother definitely had other ambitions for me. She wanted me to go to college and become a lawyer or a doctor or something.

I: Why?

A: That's a good question. I think she was like a lot of parents who want something stable and secure for their children. I don't think it had anything to do with being married to a musician herself.

I: The settled life she never had, maybe?

A: I honestly don't know. But I don't think so. Actually, she seemed to enjoy that aspect of her life—the lack of a strict routine, the unexpected visitors, late nights staying up playing music and chatting.

I: And you did go to college, but you left after a year. Was it the pull of the music world that made you leave?

A: Hmm, that's difficult to say. I don't think it was as simple as just wanting to get back to singing. I was feeling very restless at college—I wanted to travel and see more of the world.

I: And so you took off to India. Were your parents unhappy about that?

A: Do you know, I couldn't tell you really. They were very laid-back parents. Certainly in the sense that they weren't judgmental, or didn't want to be seen to be being judgmental about the things we did as kids.

I: So your first record …

A: Yes, this dates back to the time when I was traveling in India, and it's actually a bit of mass-produced pop. It's what they called *filmi*—songs that are adapted for use in Bollywood movies. It's not musically brilliant or anything, but it always makes me feel happy when I hear it.

▶ 64

F = Friend, MA = Model answer

1

F: Did music play a big part in your childhood?

MA: That's a good question. Certainly it was important in high school. Your circle of friends tended to be influenced a lot by the kind of music you listened to.

2

F: And was music a big part of family life?

MA: I've never really thought about it like that. Listening to music wasn't really something we did together as a family.

3

F: And what kind of music did your parents like?

MA: I couldn't tell you, really. My mother used to listen to the radio a lot—usually pop music from the 1960s and '70s. I don't think my father was that interested in music.

4

F: And is music still very important to you now?

MA: Hmm, I suppose so, yes. It's not the same as when I was a teenager, but I still listen to music a lot. Mostly on my computer when I'm working.

5

F: Who's your favorite singer or band?

MA: That's difficult to say. It varies from month to month. I go through stages of listening to one thing a lot, and then I change. At the moment, it's a singer named Jessie Ware.

Unit 9

▶ 65

When teacher Bruce Farrer from Regina in Canada asked students in his ninth-grade class to write letters—ten pages long—to their future selves, most of them imagined that this was just a way of keeping them busy for a few hours, and after they'd handed them in, they forgot about them. Little did they realize that twenty years later, the letters would be returned to them.

For the dedicated Farrer, however, this was an assignment with a distinct purpose. Over several decades, he handed out this same task to his fourteen- and fifteen-year-olds, knowing that twenty years later, he would endeavor to track the writers down and mail their letters back to them. Although he retired fully from teaching in 2006, Farrer kept all the letters carefully filed and has been continuing since then to return them to their owners one by one. He should finally see the job through in 2026.

Farrer says that the exercise is greatly valued by his past students, partly, he thinks, because letters are nowadays a rarer and more treasured form of communication. In the writing part of the assignment, the aim was to make students think about what they wanted to do in life and whether they were on the right track. Then, when they read them back, at the age of 35 or so, the letters had become interesting historical documents. First and foremost, says Farrer, they are just something to enjoy as you would enjoy any object that you rediscovered from your past.

Finding the students so long after they left the school has not been a straightforward job—Farrer describes it as "a lot of detective work." But the rewards are great. He gets to find out how their lives have actually evolved and, in addition, receives their gratitude for going to the trouble of returning the letters.

Not all the students agreed for him to read their

letters, but he has kept and is returning these letters, too. Most are delighted to receive them; a few are embarrassed because of the immaturity of their letters. But of those who did agree to share what they'd written, he has some interesting stories. He remembers one boy who was a big fan of the Swedish pop group ABBA. The boy's dream was to move to Sweden and marry a beautiful girl. Twenty years later, he has fulfilled his wish.

In spite of the profound effect the exercise has had on his former students, Farrer is modest about his own teaching skills, saying that he's just a regular teacher who happened to give a rather unusual assignment.

▶ 66
Archeologists working outside Vienna, Austria, believe they have discovered a huge school for ancient Roman gladiators, rivaling in size the training grounds outside Rome's Colosseum.

The facility includes features never before seen at a Roman gladiator school, such as a wooden training dummy and outside its gates, the first known gladiator cemetery.

In addition to a walled field for wild animals, it includes a mini amphitheater. Here, gladiators, who were mostly foreign slaves, could practice their moves and perform in front of potential purchasers.

▶ 67
Eight bells struck. Fletcher Christian, acting mate of His Majesty's Armed Vessel *Bounty*, came on deck to take over the watch. The ship's commander, Lieutenant William Bligh, was asleep in his cabin below.

"I am now unhappily to relate one of the most atrocious acts of piracy ever committed," Bligh later wrote. "Just before sunrise, Mr. Christian, with the master at arms, gunner's mate and seaman, Thomas Burkett, came into my cabin while I was asleep, seized me, tied my hands with a cord behind my back, and threatened me with instant death if I spoke or made the least noise. The boatswain was ordered to hoist the launch out; and some others of the crew were hurried over the side.

"Christian … then said—'Come, Captain Bligh, your officers and men are now in the boat, and you must go with them; if you attempt to make the least resistance you will instantly be put to death' and without any further ceremony, with the cord still tied around my hands and a tribe of armed ruffians about me, I was forced over the side. A few pieces of pork were thrown to us, and some clothes and cutlasses and we were cast adrift in the open ocean."

So, on April 28, 1789, began one of the greatest sea stories of all time: the mutiny on the *Bounty* and its fantastic chain of events.

Bounty had sailed from Spithead, England, in December of 1787, under orders to proceed to Tahiti, there to take on breadfruit for transport to the West Indies. She stayed nearly six months at the island taking on plants and then proceeded to Endeavour Strait by way of Tonga. There, motivated by the attractions of living in this south-sea island paradise, and by the increasing strictness and cruelty of his captain, Bligh, Fletcher Christian led the famous mutiny.

In a boat only seven meters long, heavily laden with 19 men, Bligh performed the most celebrated open-boat voyage in the chronicles of the sea. In 41 days, he sailed from Tofua to Timor, 3,618 nautical miles, without the loss of a single man. From there, he returned to England.

As the launch pulled away from the *Bounty*, the castaways heard the mutineers shout, "Huzza for Tahiti!" Christian and his mates returned to their island paradise, where sixteen of them elected to remain ashore. Then, during the night, nine of them, including Christian, plus six native men and twelve Tahitian women, sailed from Tahiti and vanished from history. Not until the ship *Topaz* of Boston landed at Pitcairn Island, a lonely rock two thousand kilometers southeast of Tahiti, eighteen years later, was the mystery solved.

Christian had taken his little band to this uninhabited island, stripped the *Bounty*, and then run her ashore and burned her. Christian knew the English Admiralty had a long arm, and that sooner or later they would send a ship to look for him and his fellow mutineers. True to his fears, the frigate *Pandora* arrived in Tahiti a year and a half later and captured all the mutineers there.

At Pitcairn, Christian's little colony lived in peace for about two years until the wife of John Williams, one of the mutineers, died in a fall from a cliff. Williams took the wife of one of the Tahitians, who banded together to take revenge. The Tahitians were already resentful that the mutineers had divided the land on Pitcairn among themselves, and there followed a series of bloody incidents. Fletcher Christian was shot to death as he worked in his field. Ten years after the *Bounty* had landed at Pitcairn, all the Tahitian men were dead, and only one mutineer, Alexander Smith, was still alive.

When Captain Mayhew Folger on the ship *Topaz* called at Pitcairn to look for seals in 1808, he was astonished to see a canoe put out to sea from what he thought was an uninhabited island. In the canoe were three young men, bearing presents of fruit and a pig. The youths took the captain ashore to meet their father, "Aleck" Smith.

To this day, Pitcairn islanders, of whom there are around fifty, are the direct descendants of these mutineers and their Tahitian friends.

▶ 68
A: How was your anthropology lecture today?
B: It was fascinating. It was about the history of eating and drinking etiquette.
A: What do you mean by "etiquette"? Like table manners?
B: Yes, exactly. We started off looking at how people in the Middle Ages behaved at the table. They

did sit at a table with a tablecloth like we do, but the cloth was a kind of communal napkin. People would wipe their hands or mouths on it. They drank soup straight from a bowl, and when they ate, they used shared knives and spoons, and just helped themselves to the meat or bread or whatever else was on the table ...

A: Are you saying that they didn't really have food served up on individual plates ... or pass food around for each other like we do?

B: That's right.

A: So, in other words, it was a bit of a free-for-all.

B: Yeah, I guess you could say that. And by today's standards it would seem very rude, but the point is that politeness is a relative thing. They did have *some* standards. For example, if they wanted to spit, they had to do it behind them, not into the tablecloth ...

A: Hmm ... great. Am I right in thinking that forks came a bit later?

B: Yes, forks didn't really become widespread until the 17th or even 18th century. And that's when napkins came in, too. It's only when you have these individual pieces of tableware that you get the evolution to the type of table manners we're more used to today.

A: So, let me get this straight. You mean that when people started to share less, then their manners started to improve?

B: I think you have to be careful using words like *improve* in this context because who's to say what's right and wrong? What I meant was that that's when we can see the beginning of modern table manners.

▶ 70

F = Friend, MA = Model answer

1
F: I saw a great program last night about the making of the modern world.
MA: What do you mean by "the making of" the modern world?

2
F: It was about how the technology of the 1980s— all the things that were invented then—changed the world we live in radically.
MA: Really? What kind of things are you talking about?

3
F: Well, for example, things like the internet, cell phones ... and also the whole consumer and shopping boom. It all really started in the '80s.
MA: Umm, correct me if I'm wrong, but didn't the internet come later than that?

4
F: Yeah, you're right. The internet wasn't actually invented till 1990. But the point is that the foundations for all these things were laid in the 1980s.
MA: And why's that important? Sorry, maybe I missed something, but I'm not sure that I really understand the significance of all this.

Unit 10

▶ 71

I = Interviewer, N = Naturalist

I: So we've talked a bit about animals that organize themselves efficiently, like ants and bees, and display the greatest collective intelligence, but which are the most social animals? I mean, which animals are the most socially aware? Which species treats other members of its group in a considerate way?

N: Oh, that would have to be the elephant—they're very considerate creatures, although I should qualify that perhaps by saying the female elephant.

I: Why's that? What about the males?

N: Well, elephant society is matriarchal—that's to say, it's the older females who lead a herd. And the older males, or bulls, live a more solitary existence. They either leave voluntarily or are pushed out of the herd when they reach maturity. One way or another, they don't remain long in the family group.

I: I see. And can you describe some of the social behavior of the main herd? What makes them socially intelligent?

N: Well, female elephants seem to form very close relationships with the other female members of the herd. This is well documented. Just to give you one recent example I read about: A young female, barely one year old, became separated from her own family and was wandering around in a disoriented way. Seeing another group nearby, she attempted to join them. This group rejected her—literally pushed her away and injured her in the process. Later, she found her own family, and the matriarch of this group recognized instantly that the young female had been the victim of some maltreatment. She seemed to put two and two together and marched straight over to the other herd and remonstrated with them. Stranger still, she seemed to know which of the elephants in the other herd had been responsible for the injury to the young female.

I: That's amazing. You'd hardly think that was possible.

N: Another example of socially cooperative behavior came in a study in Thailand, where female elephants were given a reward task. Two elephants were each given a rope. If they pulled simultaneously on their rope, a table with corn on it appeared before them. However, if one pulled their rope before the other, nothing happened. The elephants, unlike other species that have been given similar tests, learned very fast to coordinate their pulling. And this just backs up what we know about their cooperative behavior in the wild.

▶ 72

1 Research suggests that crows are able to tell the difference between one human being and another from their faces.

2 If one dolphin is sick, another will stay by it and help it breathe.

3   Meerkats can be very selfless: One will often stand watch while the others are playing or eating.
4   Young emperor penguins often group together and play together in a kind of nursery.
5   Killer whales in the northern Pacific live with their mothers all their lives.

▶ 74

P = Presenter, S = Sophie Marler

P: This week in our series *People who changed society*, we're looking at the work of peace activist Leymah Gbowee. Sophie Marler has the story.

S: In 2011, Leymah Gbowee, and Ellen Johnson Sirleaf, the first female president in Africa, were awarded the Nobel Peace Prize for their part in bringing peace to the war-torn country of Liberia. Leymah Gbowee's story is not just the story of the power of one individual to effect meaningful change in society, but of the power of collective action. Because, although Gbowee started the women's peace movement that led to the end of the civil war in 2003, without the tireless support of thousands of like-minded women, peace would likely not have come. The problem that faced Gbowee was how to reconcile different parties after years of conflict and how to begin the process of healing among victims, many of them young children. In 1998, Gbowee returned to Liberia, having fled with her three children during the civil war, and without a penny in her pocket, set about this daunting task. She volunteered on a program called the Trauma Healing and Reconciliation Program to train as a counselor and worker helping victims of war to overcome their trauma. Underpinning her philosophy was the following belief—shared by other great advocates of reconciliation like Nelson Mandela—as it is described in her book: "The person who hurt you … If you are still angry at that person, if you haven't been able to forgive, you are chained to him. When someone offends you and you haven't let go, every time you see him, you grow breathless or your heart skips a beat. Perhaps even you dream of revenge. Above you is the Mountain of Peace and Prosperity, where we all want to go. But when you try to climb that hill, the person you haven't forgiven weighs you down. It's a personal choice whether or not to let go. But you can't move forward until you break that chain."
As she trained and worked with victims of the war, she realized increasingly that this was a man's war and it was to mothers that she could most effectively appeal to end it. So she began to mobilize women across all sections of society to reconcile the different factions and in her own words to "begin the process of renewing a culture of hope" in a country where ordinary people felt hopeless. The message was that every society's future lies in its children.
In 2000, Gbowee met Thelma Ekiyor of Nigeria, an inspirational lawyer specializing in conflict resolution. Together they formed the Women in Peacebuilding Network (WIPNET) of which Gbowee became the Liberian coordinator. She continued her trauma rehabilitation work by day and by night planned actions for WIPNET. These actions were peaceful and involved groups of women going to markets and other public places and spreading the message: "Women, wake up—you have a voice in the peace process!" They handed out flyers with these words or drawings for those that could not read.
The movement grew, and soon there were mass demonstrations of women in the capital all wearing white and praying for peace. In 2003, Gbowee was granted an audience with the then-president and got him to agree to hold peace talks with the opposition. Four months later, in August 2003, the war officially came to an end. Gbowee remains a tireless campaigner and believer in the power of communities and particularly women to effect social change. She is now an internationally recognized figure spreading her message of hope around the world.

▶ 75

"The person who hurt you … If you are still angry at that person, if you haven't been able to forgive, you are chained to him. When someone offends you and you haven't let go, every time you see him, you grow breathless or your heart skips a beat. Perhaps even you dream of revenge. Above you is the Mountain of Peace and Prosperity, where we all want to go. But when you try to climb that hill, the person you haven't forgiven weighs you down. It's a personal choice whether or not to let go. But you can't move forward until you break that chain."

▶ 76

A: What are you doing?
B: Watching a TED Talk on my laptop. You know, TED—it stands for Technology, Entertainment, and Design.
A: Oh, yes. I've seen a few of those—they can be good. Which one are you looking at?
B: It's a guy named Alain de Botton. He's talking about success and failure. He's a really good speaker, actually.
A: Yes, he is, isn't he? I heard him on the radio a few months ago being interviewed about a new book. He was excellent. So what's he saying?
B: Well, he's putting forward an interesting idea: that we all think that meritocracy in society is a good thing, because it means that those who deserve to get to the top will get to the top, rather than just the rich or the well-connected.
A: Yeah, well, I'd go along with that.
B: Hmm, me too, but what he's saying is that if you believe that, then you'll also believe that those who get to the bottom, or those who just are at the bottom of society, also deserve to be there—and to stay there.
A: Oh, yes, I suppose so. I hadn't thought about it like that before.

B: No, me neither. It's interesting, isn't it? So the idea is that if you fail somehow, you've deserved to fail—it's your own fault. And he's saying that that can be pretty crushing for people.

A: Yes, I see, when in fact it might not be your fault at all. It might be because of some misfortune or bad luck.

B: Exactly.

A: So what does he suggest we do about it?

B: Well, that we change our attitudes about people who don't succeed; that we don't make judgments about them, calling them "losers" and things like that. Should I send you the link?

A: Yes, do. I'd like to watch it. Is it very long?

B: I haven't gotten to the end yet, but I doubt it. They're usually only about fifteen minutes or so.

A: Thanks. Anyway, why did I stop by? Ah, yes. I wanted to ask you about going to the …

▶ 77

1   A: What are you doing?
    B: Watching a TED Talk on my laptop.
2   A: He's a really good speaker, actually.
    B: Yes, he is, isn't he?
3   B: Yeah, well, I'd go along with that.
    A: Hmm, me too.
4   B: I hadn't thought about it like that before.
    A: No, me neither.
5   A: And he's saying that that can be pretty crushing for people.
    B: Yes, I see.
6   A: Should I send you the link?
    B: Yes, do.
7   B: Is it very long?
    A: I haven't gotten to the end yet, but I doubt it.

▶ 78

1   Doubt it.
2   'Xpect so.
3   'Fraid not.
4   S'pose so.
5   S'a good idea, isn't it?

▶ 79

F = Friend, MA = Model answer
1
F1: What are you doing this evening?
MA: Staying in, I think.
2
F2: I'm reading a really interesting book at the moment.
MA: Really? What's it about?
3
F1: Two hundred years ago, French wasn't the only language spoken in France.
MA: Wasn't it? What did they speak, then?
4
F2: I don't normally read history books.
MA: No, me neither. But your book sounds interesting.
5
F1: Are you going to be free later?
MA: No, I'm afraid not. I have too much work to do.

Unit 11

▶ 80

In Japan, there are estimated to be over half a million young people who have withdrawn from society and sit at home in the safety of their bedrooms, fearing what lies outside. These are the hikikomori. Many feel pity for them, believing that it is a symptom of a dysfunctional society. Others say it is self-indulgent and it's high time that these young people pulled themselves together.

Most hikikomori are male, and many come from middle-class families—families who do their best to help them. But their children are locked in a cycle of depression and loss of confidence. Mostly, they would prefer their parents just leave them alone to sit in their rooms and watch television or browse the internet; or just to sit doing nothing in their state of isolation.

The hikikomori condition was first formally recognized by Japanese psychiatrist Tamaki Saito in 1998 in his book *Social Withdrawal: A Never-Ending Adolescence*, and although there have been some similar cases reported in France and other Western countries, it seems to be a particularly Japanese phenomenon.

Some say that it has to do with today's uncertain economic prospects. Thirty years ago, young middle-class Japanese males trod a fairly sure path from high school to university to a job for life in one of Japan's corporations. Anyone who didn't take this route was considered abnormal. Nowadays, more graduates compete for fewer jobs and companies are less inclined to offer long-term employment. Hence, some wonder why, when they have done everything right, do they now find themselves without a good or secure job. They are confused and lost, and many end up wishing they had not worked so hard for this empty dream in the first place.

Others blame the parents, high achievers in their own careers, whose success the young hikikomori wish they could emulate. Unable to face the disappointment of their children not finding job security, the parents instead enable them to live this reclusive life. If only the parents would act more firmly, these critics say, instead of shielding them from the outside world, the problem would not exist.

Whatever the true causes, this is both a personal and a social problem that needs to be addressed; somehow these lost souls need to be reintegrated into society and re-socialized.

▶ 83

OK, so here's my dilemma. I've been offered a fantastic job in Australia, 10,000 kilometers away from where I live now. The problem is that my parents are in their eighties, and I'm the only one in the family who still lives near them. If I took the job, I wouldn't be able to see them more than once or twice a year. Should anything happen to them while I was in Australia, I'd feel terrible. But at the same time, I don't know if I will ever get an opportunity like this again. Were I to tell them, they'd of course say that I must go, but it's not that simple.

 84

Part 1

With the exception of the odd robot dog or pet cat, robotics research has, for the most part, been confined to what robots can do to simulate human activity: driving trains, performing industrial operations, even doing household chores. But a team of engineers at Harvard University, who saw a TV program called *Silence of the Bees* about the decline of the honey bee population, was inspired to create "RoboBee," a miniature flying robot that could replicate the flying skills and behavior of a real honey bee. The application they had in mind for RoboBee was the important function of pollinating crops that the shortage of honey bees has made a necessity.

The scientists have great ambitions for RoboBee. Rob Wood, Gu-Yeon Wei, and Radhika Nagpal hope to create colonies of RoboBees that will be able to work together in much the same way that a real bee colony does. In other words, they would like to simulate the collective intelligence of real bees. In this way, the small robots will be able to cooperate on a particular task, share information, and adapt to changing conditions. Artificial sensors will help them react to the movement of objects and other RoboBees around them.

Part 2

However, RoboBee faces several technical challenges before it can get to this stage. The first is flying properly. RoboBee has an intricate computer chip brain that works like a nervous system, telling the bee when to flap its wings, what direction to tilt its body, and so on. Real bees are amazing flying machines, zipping from one flower to another and then hovering there while they collect pollen. At the moment, RoboBee crashes a bit too frequently. Another problem is powering the small robot. The fuel source cannot be too heavy, or it will impede RoboBee's ability to fly. A collaborator is working on micro fuel cells that could be used instead of batteries. In the future, the team hopes that they will be able to re-create a real bee hive, which the small robots will use as a refueling station.

Perhaps the most exciting thing about coordinated robotic insects is the variety of purposes for which they can be used. RoboBees can't make honey like real bees, but they can autonomously pollinate fields of crops. Other proposed applications for RoboBees include: search and rescue missions following natural disasters—for example, searching for survivors in collapsed buildings following an earthquake; traffic monitoring—this involves flying over a traffic-congested area and taking pictures to determine the severity and the cause of the jam; weather mapping—again using cameras and other sensors in place of eyes and antennae, RoboBees could relay real-time information about weather conditions in a particular area; evaluating or exploring areas that are dangerous for humans to enter, like a nuclear reactor; and military surveillance.

Part 3

Bees, in fact, are not alone in providing inspiration for roboticists. Flies, fish, and lobsters have also been the subject of study as scientists attempt to take lessons from nature and apply them to the robot world. It's believed that in the coming years, such study will open up a wide range of discoveries and practical innovations, helping us to create a new generation of machines that will take advantage of the designs of nature and the principles that animals apply in the complex task of daily survival. The National Science Foundation in the United States is certainly convinced of the potential benefits and is funding such research to the tune of $2 million per year.

 85
See ▶ 84 Part 1

▶ 86
See ▶ 84 Part 2

▶ 87
See ▶ 84 Part 3

▶ 88

Conversation 1

A: You look a little taken aback. I didn't mean to offend you during the meeting when I said that I didn't like your ideas for changing the website.
B: No, that's OK. You're perfectly entitled to give your opinion. I was just a bit surprised because yesterday when I showed you my ideas, you said they were good.
A: Yes, they are good ideas, but I don't think they're really appropriate for what we're trying to achieve. Anyway, I'm sorry if that came out wrong at the meeting.
B: I just wish you'd been clearer yesterday before I proposed them to everyone.

Conversation 2

A: You seem worried. Is something bothering you?
B: Yes, it is, actually. You shouldn't have spoken to Sarah about my feelings about my new job.
A: Did I say something to upset you?
B: Yes, you told her that I wasn't really happy working in the back office.
A: Well, you aren't, are you?
B: No, I'm not. But I don't want her to think that I'm a whiner or someone who can't put up with a little routine paperwork.
A: Oh, well, I'm sorry. I really hope I didn't give her that impression.

Conversation 3

A: Sorry, why are you laughing? I don't understand what's so funny.
B: Nothing. It was just the way you said "no" so sharply to Gary when he asked you if you wanted to go with him to the trade fair.

A: Sorry, maybe that sounded a little abrupt.
B: No, it's OK. He's very thick-skinned. I don't think he would have minded. Anyway, everyone knows where you stand now.

▶ 91

C = Colleague, MA = Model answer

1
C: Well, I'm a little surprised that you volunteered me for the project.
MA: Oh, I'm sorry. I hope I didn't upset you. I didn't mean to put you in a difficult situation.

2
C: You look worried. Is everything OK? Was it something I said?
MA: No, don't worry. I'm just feeling a little anxious about all the work I have to do.

3
C: If you don't like Indian food, you don't have to accept my invitation to lunch.
MA: Oh, no, it's not that. Please don't think I'm rude. It's just that I don't eat lunch normally.

4
C: Ha, ha, that's a good one.
MA: Why are you laughing? I don't understand what's so funny.

5
C: Is that all you have to say: "No"?

MA: Sorry, maybe that sounded a little abrupt. I should have said, "No, I don't think that's likely to be a good technical solution."

Unit 12

▶ 92

I = Interviewer, M = Marie
I: You immigrated to the United States as a child. How did your love for the landscape in South America affect your relationship with North America?
M: I grew up on a sugarcane hacienda outside Trujillo, Peru, on the coast of the Pacific Ocean, so as a child, I was always aware of the land and the sea. My earliest memories are of earthquakes—there were over fifteen by the time I reached the age of five. When I came to North America, I was struck by how much of the land around me was inhabited. I couldn't imagine a place where you could drive for hundreds of miles and human beings always be in evidence.
I: What landscapes in North America do you love?
M: The first memorable impression I had was the smell of cut grass. Having grown up in a kind of desert, I had never seen great fields of grass. I loved that.
I: What is your favorite landscape in South America?
M: Most people don't know this, but Peru has five kinds of landforms: coastal desert, mountain, jungle, islands, and prairie. And all of it in close-ish proximity! It always amazes me that you can descend a snow-covered mountain not far from Cuzco and suddenly be in the lush, green jungle. I love it.

I: How did flying with photographer Bobby Haas for this project change your understanding of South America?
M: In all truth, I was taken aback by the growth of the cities. The urban centers have burgeoned as countryfolk sought refuge from earthquakes, famines, and floods. Seeing the shantytowns that had sprouted up around the cities in the past thirty years or so was heartbreaking. But on the positive side, I was moved to see the prevailing beauty of the land. I had never imagined it could look like that. The sights from around 1,500 meters in the air were astoundingly beautiful!
I: What was it like to ride in an open-door airplane? Was it a thrill, or just terrifying?
M: I was both thrilled and terrified! Terrified by how vulnerable some small airplane can feel and thrilled by the visual feast below us. But what made the greatest impression on me was the physical aspect: fierce gales rushing through the open door and the cold. It's freezing. How Bobby was able to handle his camera and manipulate stuff under those conditions is still a mystery to me.

▶ 93

1 A: Where do you live now?
   B: We've moved to a city in Jordan called Irbid, about 100 kilometers north of the capital.
2 A: Is that near where you work?
   B: It's close-ish. Getting to work at the university takes me thirty minutes or so.
3 A: What's the countryside like around there?
   B: It's farmland mostly, but not very rich. Some people would call it sparse, but I kind of like it.
4 A: Are you near the desert?
   B: The desert is to the east, some distance away, but we haven't visited it yet. I'd love to go sometime, but there's so much other stuff to see that we haven't gotten around to it.

▶ 95

As cities grow and natural habitats for animals shrink, one of two things is going to happen: Either wild animal populations will decrease because people won't be able to live *with* them, or people can adapt their ways and try to accommodate animals living among them. In Europe, for example, people seem to have gotten used to urban foxes.

Now, obviously, some animals are easier to live with than others. I'm a big fan of tigers, and I'd be devastated if their numbers grew so small that in the end they only existed in zoos and safari parks. At the same time, much as I love them, I don't really want to live next to a tiger, let alone a lot of them. You'd think the same would probably go for most people. Yet some of the tribes of the Western Ghats mountains have shown that co-existence with tigers is not only possible, it's positively healthy.

Encouragingly, in 2016 the number of tigers in the world actually rose—that was the first time in over 100 years that it had—and now stands at around

4,000. And in the Western Ghats in India, the population has almost doubled in recent years. That's because the local tribes there don't hunt tigers and they don't compete with them for food either, given that most are vegetarian (the people that is, not the tigers). In fact, for farmers of vegetable and cereal crops, the presence of tigers is beneficial because they keep other crop-eating animals under control. One of the tribes, the Soliga, even worship tigers as gods and claim they haven't had any kind of conflict with tigers for years.

But, ironically, a lot of the tribes living in India's western nature reserves are now being evicted and relocated. This is being done in the name of safety *and* conservation of the natural areas and wild animals; some also worry that the indigenous people might be tempted to poach tigers illegally for their valuable skins. Yet the fact remains that these are the very people who have made tiger conservation a success.

We need to recognize that the historic residents of these areas—and probably of similar natural areas all over the world—make the best conservationists. They understand the land, their environmental footprint is very light, and most importantly, they respect other living things that co-habit with them. We need to keep them there—whether by giving aid or just leaving them alone—rather than evicting them. Keeping people in tiger reserves may, on the surface, seem like a cruel thing to do, but actually, it's the best chance that the tigers have of survival.

▶ 96

H = Harry, C = Cynthia, S = Stefano
H: Hi, Cynthia. Hi, Stefano. Mind if I join you?
C: Oh, hi, Harry. No, not at all. We were just discussing the new golf course they're planning to build along the beachfront.
H: Oh, yes. I'm not so sure about that.
C: Of course, Stefano thinks it's a great idea because he loves golf and …
S: Sorry, can I just interrupt you there? It's not for selfish reasons. I just happen to think golf courses can be very attractive places. And in this area of coast …
C: Yes, but they're exclusive. Only a few rich people get to use them.
S: Well, that's not true, but can I just finish what I was saying? In this area of coast, there are plenty of places—beautiful places—for walkers to enjoy the scenery. But there are very few places where people can play sports. So I don't see why you would oppose the idea of giving people a chance to practice their hobby or sport, because you feel that …
H: No, sorry. I have to stop you there, Stefano. I'm afraid I agree with Cynthia. This is an area of outstanding natural beauty, and it's not right to make it exclusive when at the moment it can be enjoyed by everyone.
S: Actually, the land will be much better looked after when it's made into a golf course. The grass

will be cut, the area will be landscaped in a much more attractive way, and …
C: Can I just say something in answer to that? That misses the point completely. This is an area of natural beauty, not of man-made beauty. This is a kind of environmental vandalism.
S: No, hold on a minute. That's a completely inappropriate description. Golf courses actually protect the landscape against other kinds of development.
H: Well, I wouldn't …
S: Harry, you can make your point in a moment. If you put a golf course here, it's a kind of guarantee that no one else is going to develop the land in some other less environmentally friendly way.
H: They're not actually that environmentally friendly. Do you have any idea how much water it takes to keep a golf course going and how much energy they use?

▶ 98
Can I just finish what I was saying?

▶ 99
F = Friend, MA = Model answer
1
F: I was very pleased to hear about the new golf course. Were you?
MA: No, I wasn't, actually. I don't see why they have to build it in a national park.
2
F: Well, it's not as if they're building a shopping mall or anything. Golf courses are naturally beautiful places with lots of …
MA: Sorry, I have to stop you there. They are not natural. They're man-made, and they change the landscape.
3
F: Yes, but not in a bad way. If anything, they make it more beautiful to walk around.
MA: Well, they do for a few people who can afford to belong to a golf club. But for most people, they are inaccessible.
4
F: Anyway, we need more sports facilities in the area. I imagine it will encourage more people, not fewer, to visit the area.
MA: Hang on a minute. Lots of people already visit the area: walkers, cyclists, families …
5
F: Can I just finish what I was saying?
MA: Sure, go on.